The
NEW Science
of LOVE

The NEW Science of LOVE

HOW UNDERSTANDING YOUR
BRAIN'S WIRING CAN HELP
Rekindle YOUR RELATIONSHIP

Dr. Fran
Cohen Praver

Foreword by
Paul E. Bendheim, MD

sourcebooks
casablanca

Published by Sourcebooks Casablanca, an imprint of Sourcebooks, Inc.
P.O. Box 4410, Naperville, Illinois 60567-4410
(630) 961-3900
Fax: (630) 961-2168
www.sourcebooks.com

Library of Congress Cataloging-in-Publication Data

Praver, Frances Cohen.
  The new science of love : how understanding your brain's wiring can help rekindle your relationship / by Fran Cohen Praver.
      p. cm.
    1. Love. 2. Intimacy (Psychology) 3. Psychophysiology. 4. Interpersonal relations. 5. Man-woman relationships. I. Title.
  BF575.L8P73 2011
  158.2--dc22
                        2011007318

Printed and bound in the United States of America.
    VP 10 9 8 7 6 5 4 3 2 1

*To the loving memory of Bessie and Sam and
the loving presence of Vicky and Leland*

contents

Foreword

By Paul E. Bendheim, MD

Author of *The Brain Training Revolution: A Proven Workout for Healthy Brain Aging*

Welcome to the new science of love. You have opened an enlightening "love book," but not in the usual romantic sense. The beginning chapters here are insightful, understandable descriptions of aspects of modern brain science: how this revolutionary new science of the *changeable* adult brain explains our ability to understand and communicate effectively again with a once-cherished partner, to regain the luster of love diminished, and then to maintain its recaptured magic. In the following sections, we are expertly guided through real-life examples and specific mental exercises to harness these intrinsic brain capabilities for rebuilding a damaged relationship. We can arrive again at that treasured place that feeling and thinking men and women rank among their highest priorities: an intimate, respectful, invigorating relationship with our life partner.

Every aspect of our personalities, ambitions, and

abilities to relate to others in the most profound manner reside in one place and one place only: our brain. As William James, the founder of modern psychology, put it more than one hundred years ago, "The greatest discovery of my generation is that a human being can alter his life by altering his attitude." We now know, based on discoveries made in the past several decades, that the adult brain contains "mirror neurons" whose connections are not hardwired. This means that your mature brain can actually generate new cells and new connections; it can physically change. In our daily lives, the approach we take to life and life's problems—our concerted mental efforts—can rewire the brain networks responsible for our most important human interactions: communicating, understanding, empathizing, and loving.

The science of how each of us subconsciously understands what our partner perceives, thinks, and feels has been propelled forward by the monumental discovery of the brain's mirror neurons made barely fifteen years ago. These brain cells have been labeled "monkey see, monkey do" cells, as they were first discovered in experimental monkeys. The same brain cells are active when the monkey performs an action or when she simply witnesses another performing this action.

In the human brain, mirror neurons are now the subject of intense and widespread research and theorizing. They may be the central actors in those vast networks, connecting billions of brain cells, that allowed the breathtakingly

rapid (in evolutionary terms) advance of human culture.
V. S. Ramachandran speculates that "mirror neurons will do for psychology what DNA did for biology: they will provide a unifying framework and help explain a host of mental abilities that have hitherto remained mysterious and inaccessible to experiments." Mirror neurons seem to be involved in verbal and nonverbal communication, language, imitation or mimicry, socialization, our ability to understand others, and, as Dr. Praver bravely asserts, our ability to forgive, to be forgiven, and to love again.

Dr. Praver's book, though based on brain science, is not a neuroscience text. She uses the brain's intrinsic plasticity and the role of mirror neurons in human verbal and nonverbal communications and empathy as a springboard to help all of us who have experienced difficulties in love. Employing the knowledge gained from her many years of experience as a practicing psychologist specializing in couples therapy, she leads us down that challenging yet ultimately rewarding road of repairing a damaged relationship. The honesty with which she emphasizes the hard work required is refreshing for a book of this genre. There is no magic bullet, but the goal of rekindling the magic of love you once had for your partner is achievable. If you and your partner diligently practice Dr. Praver's clinically proven methods, you will change your brain and enjoy a healthier, happier, lustier love life.

Acknowledgments

The impetus for this book began in my practice, where I see couples who try to bring intimacy back into their relationships. To all of the brave souls who have entered into therapy with me, I thank you. I am awed by your inner strengths and marvel at how you have succeeded in experiencing once again the ecstasy of passionate love.

I owe my training in psychoanalytic theory to my esteemed professors at the Gordon F. Derner postdoctoral program at Adelphi University. The program offered me a warm, accepting environment for exploring the fantasies, symbolic meanings, and real experiences of intimate relationships, along with their scientific underpinnings. The research professors at St. John's University, where I obtained my PhD, whetted my curiosity for delving into the intricacies of science, research, and their life applications.

I am deeply indebted to my son, Leland; his wife,

Vicky; and my analyst, Roberta Jellinek, PhD—they have always believed in me all the way. From this amalgam of cherished people—professors, mentors, colleagues, and family—I have been inspired to derive the therapies that I have used successfully with my patients. Also, my literary agent Katherine Flynn's generous and expert guidance is priceless. Shana Drehs, my editor at Sourcebooks, has been on track with me from the beginning and continues to guide and inspire me.

My clinical and research experiences presented me with an urgent cry to share my knowledge with a wider audience—all of you who want to bring intimacy back into your lives.

Introduction

The photograph came from another era, the story it told long forgotten. There they were, honeymoon lovers, high on a promontory over a bright blue ocean, looking out on a shining future. Kathy and Ken were young, slender, and vibrant. Their hair tossed in the breeze, their arms were around each other in a full embrace, and they gazed into each other's eyes.

Behind the scenes, the remarkable power of the brain was in play. Mirror neurons—minuscule brain cells that, at an internal level, connect two people who are in a meaningful relationship—linked Kathy and Ken in the most thrilling, spiritual, and sensual experience. Feelings of love, lust, and loyalty flooded them. On that promontory, with matching mirror neurons, each member of the couple reflected inner needs, desires, intentions, and goals to the other. In doing so, their mirror neurons triggered the release of brain chemicals to ensure those ecstatic feelings. Almost instantly a cascade of love-inducing brain chemicals and good-mood neurotransmitters bathed Kathy and Ken. Madly in love, they reflected to each other the promise of a fulfilling and lasting love.

Twenty-five years after that picture was taken, Kathy and Ken sat before me. Gray roots were visible under Kathy's carefully upswept hair, and Ken's once-wavy locks were thinning dramatically. Both of their frames seemed heavier. Ken grimaced in pain as he crossed his legs, and I could see the start of arthritis swelling in the knuckles on Kathy's hands. All these were simply signs of aging—natural, normal, inevitable.

But simple aging had not brought this couple to my office; rather, it was the loss of the passion that the honeymoon photograph showed so clearly and vividly. Kathy and Ken were simply no longer madly in love. Mirror neurons that once activated the brain systems that stored happy memories and hopeful wishes now activated those that stored old wounds, painful interactions, and feelings of despair.

"When did the love fade?" Kathy wondered aloud. "Ten years ago? Twenty? Last week?" Ken couldn't remember, either; he knew only that they had traveled a long way from the boundless ardor of their honeymoon photograph—a vibrant, bright fire had turned to fading embers. Love-inducing chemicals and good-mood neurotransmitters ceased to flow in the relationship; the vitality of love sputtered.

As Kathy and Ken talked, their feelings emerged.
Although they still cared for each other in some way, their
relationship had badly frayed. Kathy was hurt; Ken was
uncomprehending. Kathy felt damaged; Ken felt rejected.
Anger, resentment, and despair flew through the air. She
said he was controlling and imperious; he charged that
she was indifferent and frigid, that she wasn't really trying to mend the marriage. They talked past each other,
out of sync, and their frustration and sense of injury
drove their words.

They were two people clearly bonded, attached by history, circumstance, even by a shared desire for change.
They wanted to bring love back, but, unable to let go of
past hurts, they simply didn't know how or where to begin
and didn't know if they could even do so.

I'm here to tell you it *can* be done. Before I do that,
though, let me tell you a little about me. Over the years,
as a clinical psychologist and a psychoanalyst, I have
immersed myself in the study of the anatomy of the brain
and how it functions in relationships. An understanding
of unconscious processes, both within ourselves and in
our relationships, and an exploration of neuroscience have
enriched my understanding not only of why people repeat
problematic interactions but also of how to help them create deep, lasting change on a neural basis. For twelve of
my twenty years of private practice, I have helped couples
in therapy create change in their relationships by applying
the principles of neuroscience. For example, knowing that

the brain is plastic and can reshape itself has given hope to many couples and has helped them positively alter the conditions that are conducive to relationship repair.

Falling in love and being loved in return is the peak experience of human existence. It's what everyone wants—to become the object of a beloved's longing. That is why, when love falters and hurtful relationships erode our selfhood, it feels so much as if we are taking a painful and debilitating downward plunge. Until recently, we've assumed that mysterious forces or chance drove these tides of human emotion and that romantic relationships would remain enigmas—to be fathomed by poets, if at all.

Science tells another story, however. Exciting discoveries point to the incredible power that mirror neurons—the tiny brain cells that connect two partners' internal worlds and simultaneously connect to their own multifunctioning brain systems—have on our love lives. Specifically, these brain systems that neuroscientists have analyzed indicate that mirror neurons, these infinitesimal brain cells, are wired to our functions of memory, feelings, empathy, memory, nonverbal communication, intentions, sensation, and perception. When these mirror neurons "fire," or are activated, they trigger connections and associations that flash across neural pathways. When applied to relationships, this process quite literally explains how and why two people, like Kathy and Ken, or your partner and yourself, fall in love with each other, fall out of love, and can bring love back.

The brain, in short, is the real heart of love, and the mirror neurons its beating pulse. Does knowing this reduce love to a mechanical series of engineering functions? Not at all. On the contrary, research on mirror neurons illuminates the concept that we are inherently programmed from birth to bond, to attach, to empathize, and to tune into one another at an emotional level (often called attunement). By tuning into one another, we can actually empathize with feelings that are dissimilar to our own, so that we can take someone else's perspective. And doing so is what real acceptance and intimacy are about. Studies have revealed that our brains drive us to connect—in other words, that we are wired for love. After all, love coupled with lust is the basis of our survival as a species.

Implicit in that research is the inspirational message of this book: when love fades, we can quite literally use our brains to bring it back. By learning how to rewire your mirror neurons, you will reactivate the associations and brain chemicals that first triggered communication, empathy, attunement, and erotic experience with your partner—the initial springboards to love in your relationship. You also will feel hopeful; you will dislodge painful relationship interactions from the brain and make room for fresh interactions of love.

In an intimate relationship, mirror neurons help link partners in a fluid psychological and neural system. And it takes only one person to make a change in the system. Does that mean that one person can single-handedly change the entire dynamic of a relationship? Not exactly. It does mean, however, that when we become empowered and create change in ourselves, our partners—whose impulses are linked to our own by their matching mirror neurons—are more likely to change as well.

As powerful as mirror neurons that connect partners are, they are not a cure-all. And change in one partner does not guarantee change in the other; rather, it takes the determination and persistence of both partners to create new loving conditions that are more conducive to bringing back intimacy. Relationship changes occur on a two-way street of hard work by both partners. Unfortunately, no matter how hard one person tries to change, the other partner may refuse to put in the work to change him- or herself. Hopefully, your partner does share your wish to revive the relationship and will climb on board with you. As you modify how you relate to your partner, there is a far greater chance that your partner will modify how he or she relates to you.

Does this mean that you and your partner have a good chance of rekindling the embers of a relationship gone cold? That with work you can change a dynamic of damage into one of positivity, wholesomeness, and restoration? That your faded love can once again burn brightly? That even as you age, you can recharge the intense passion of the early days? That your partner and you can once again set your bodies, minds, and souls soaring? Yes, that's exactly what it means!

Understanding the biology and chemistry of love—how

love comes, fades, and revives—is the foundation of this book. Through a series of step-by-step exercises based in that science, you will learn how to harness the power of your brain to stockpile the skills you need to deal with relationship problems. Armed with these skills, you can actually help "rewire" your partner's brain, and you will learn how to attack negative relationship dynamics and replace them with positive, intimate ones.

Now let's go back to Kathy and Ken to see how they harnessed the power of their brains to change their dynamics of pain back to those of love. When Kathy reflected on her past, she encountered none other than her overbearing, critical mother, who told her what to do, when to do it, and how to do it. "I married my mother," she said, wincing. "Ken is so controlling, just like my mother was." In therapy, we dug a little deeper to learn that, as a child, Kathy complied with her mother's dictates and, in so doing, lost her own sense of self-mastery. Hampered by feelings of inadequacy, she grew up feeling dependent, insecure, and effectively unable to make decisions for herself.

Ken was a strong, independent man who had always made all the decisions, whether or not Kathy liked it. When things did not go as Ken had planned, Ken blamed Kathy, who attacked right back. Kathy had devolved into a depressed, withdrawn woman whose desires for intimacy had diminished. As for Ken, his feelings of rejection and sexual frustration had filled him with rage. Their marriage had lost its magic; it was not working.

In order to rewire the neural pathways in her brain and reactivate those love-inducing chemicals, Kathy needed to address her childhood relationships. By reflecting on her past, Kathy learned that the script she followed back then—that of a controlling mother and a submissive child—was playing out anew in her relationship with Ken. Her insight propelled her to change how she felt about herself so that she could live and love better in the present. She also felt hopeful that with hard work, when she changed her patterns of relating to Ken, her mirror neurons would reflect this change to Ken's mirror neurons so that he would be more likely to make changes to how he related to her as well.

Before Kathy could feel independent and autonomous and have the confidence to make decisions, she began to work on ways to build her self-esteem. She visualized Michelle Obama—a powerful woman whom she admired—and tried to imagine herself as a strong woman who articulated her needs and desires. She then imagined herself as a more powerful, more assertive woman, both at home with Ken and at her job. Kathy joined a gym, began a vigorous endorphin-enhancing aerobic dance class, and met other fun and supportive women.

Initially, her newfound strengths met with some resistance from Ken, so the two embarked on some interactive exercises to better communicate verbally and nonverbally. They then learned how to empathize with each other, to feel remorse for inflicting pain on the other, and to finally forgive one another for having caused such pain. Before long, Kathy was more comfortable in her skin (she even got a promotion at work!), and Ken was enjoying his more lively and engaged wife. They then began to address some of the hurtful interactions they were engaged in, such as their unequal division of power and Kathy's tendency to disconnect love from lust. On their road to recovery, their mirror neurons began to again reflect more empathy, emotional attunement, and intimacy with each other. Kathy's sex drive reignited, as did Ken's tender, loving side.

Kathy and Ken are one of many couples in this book with whom you can identify. By seeing how those couples have applied the theories of mirror neurons to restore love and lust in their relationships, I hope you will be inspired to do the same.

Let's take a quick look at what you'll find in this book.

THE NEW NEUROSCIENCE

In part 1, we'll get up close and personal with the freshest and most exciting discoveries in neuroscience: mirror neurons. By applying the principles found in mirror neurons to relationships, we'll see how mirror neurons connect partners in intimate relationships and how love-inducing brain chemicals—aided by mirror neurons—reflect one person's attraction, romance, love, lust, and loyalty to his or her partner.

By understanding the neural underpinnings of love, you

will see how you can restore your relationship. The brain has infinite capacity to change, which is known as neural plasticity. And so we can take advantage of that plasticity to repair the negative patterns that seem to be hardwired into our brains and thus repair a faltering relationship. Infant-mother studies show that, from the get-go, mirror neurons lay the groundwork for empathy, reciprocity, and emotional attunement. The studies focus on the seamless synchronization of nonverbal communication between infants and mothers. Change in one affects change in the other. These studies imply that we have the inherent ability to change others. If you and your partner follow the prescriptions in this book and are both determined to change, then you very likely will.

REWIRING, REPAIRING, AND REVIVING

Before you can tackle a crumbling relationship, you must acquire some essential tools, which you'll find in part 2. You will learn skills to empower you to create new interactions so that you and your partner "get" each other all over again—skills for reflecting on the past, living in the present, empowering yourself, communicating, stirring empathy, feeling remorse, forgiving, and triggering emotional attunement.

In each and every hurtful interaction in a relationship, inevitably, one partner feels diminished. I prescribe steps to develop a more independent, confident, secure, vital sense of self, as well as a whole set of prescriptions that embody the kinds of therapies I use with patients in my practice every day. As an operating manual, part 2 empowers you to focus on love instead of pain, and to reflect those things onto your partner.

TACKLING HURTFUL INTERACTIONS AND RESTORING LOVE

With the tools from part 2, in part 3 you are ready to tackle the repetitive, hurtful interactions that link you and your partner. When you remove the hurtful emotional obstacles that have become lodged in your brain, you make room for new loving interactions—and the return of empathy, emotional attunement, romance, love, and lust. In part 3, you will learn how to tackle relationship traps such as unequal power sharing, which sets up the pernicious dynamic of domination and submission, and negative fortune-telling, during which partners unwittingly provoke each other to act out their worst traits. You'll then learn how you and your partner can rekindle the flame of desire by connecting love and lust for an erotic, loving relationship. In this healing process, you and your partner will create new neural patterns and revive real intimacy.

- ♡ -

Simply put, when you change how you love, you change how your brain is wired. The riveting scientific underpinnings of *The New Science of Love* will help you bring intimacy back into your life. That is not to say that *The New Science of Love* is the only brain book out there. Browse any bookstore and you will find a wide range of titles promising to help you retrain your brain to become smarter, to lower stress and raise confidence, to end anxiety and calm your emotions, to succeed better at work and beat the competition in business, to get organized, to get rich, to lose weight, and even to have a better church life. However, this is the first book to show you how to use your brain to heal and enhance what is perhaps the most essential and universal of human experiences—the intimate relationship.

Throughout the book, case studies illustrate how couples have used science-based strategies in therapy to rewire their brains and revive their relationships. To protect these couples' confidentiality, I have disguised their identities. The case studies are composites of multiple patients, as are their relationships with each other and with me, their therapist.

Let's get started.

Part One

The New Neuroscience: The Brain Is the Heart of Love and Mirror Neurons Its Beating Pulse

Chapters 1 and 2 briefly discuss the scientific basis of mirror neurons that underlies relationship repair. The cutting-edge research on mirror neurons, a special type of brain cell, is riveting in and of itself. Most important, mirror neurons create bonds of empathy, emotional attunement, and reciprocity between people.

In these chapters, you will read about some fascinating infant-mother studies that reveal just how love emerges and how mirror neurons trigger emotional attunement and shared experience, which combine to form the launching pad not only of parental love but also of romantic love.

Captivating research and case studies of real couples work-ing through their relationship problems will show more clearly the effect that mirror neurons have on our love lives.

By understanding the brain-based underpinnings of love and the phenomenon of mirror neurons, you will learn that, although intimate partners who speak of feel-ing like "two strands of a single thread" may be speaking in metaphors, they are articulating a scientific fact: mirror neurons link the unconscious minds of those who are in love. When you "get" your partner, he or she "gets" you. That kind of mutual attunement creates a bond that is the most satisfying thing we know, so satisfying that we hope and believe that it is eternal.

Alas, things have a way of changing. Perhaps present reality fails to live up to the core of happy memories our mirror neurons activated, or perhaps the hopeful associa-tions that the mirror neurons triggered aren't met. Over time, interactions of love become interactions of pain.

The remarkable quality of mirror neurons has a down-side, too. We cause damage and hurt, and the hurt fires our mirror neurons just as good feelings do. Mirror neu-rons (that are a subset of multiple types of other neurons) can trigger old pain, light up sad associations, and wire us to emotionally difficult and unhappy scenarios. Such associations—many from painful childhood relationships that we acted out with family members—color our adult relationships. Love-inducing brain chemicals, which mir-ror neurons once triggered, cease to flow, and romance is on the rocks. You believe your relationship cannot be restored, and it feels like the end of love.

It needn't be so. The brain is extraordinarily plastic; it can be shaped and formed, reshaped and reformed.[1] Change your interactions, and you can change the way your mirror neurons are wired. This rewiring in you, in turn, will reflect onto your partner. Because you are both linked by mirror neurons, once you change—with insight into and work on relationship problems—there is greater likelihood that your partner will also change.

Chapter 1

unraveling the Mystery of Mirror Neurons

Empathy, Emotional Attunement, and Intimacy

Understanding how love works provides hope and empowers you to revive your relationship and once again have a meeting of minds, souls, and bodies. Learning about the neurobiology of intimacy will give you hope that, when love is teetering on the brink, you can strengthen it and re-create a vibrant, lasting love. In this chapter, you will learn about how the mirror neuron system provides the infrastructure[2] for empathy, emotional attunement, intimacy, and the nonverbal communication of one another's feelings, perceptions, goals, and intentions—the keys to a passionate love life.

MIRROR NEURONS

Brain cells called neurons are activated (or fired) when we perform an action. However, mirror neurons, unique brain cells located in the premotor cortex, fire not only when we perform an action but also when we observe someone else performing an action.[3] Our mirror neurons reflect, or create a mirror image of, someone else's behavior, emotions, and sensations in our brains, and we can relate to that image as though it were our own.

Mirror neurons function in two ways simultaneously: they are activated by another person's behavior and internal life, and at the same time they trigger your internal events, such as past trauma, memories, feelings, and nonverbal communication.[4] That's because mirror neurons, which are visual/motor neurons, are a subset of a large group of multimodal neurons—neurons that function in various ways. Multimodal neurons connect to sensations, perceptions, emotions, memories, and auditory, olfactory, and visual stimuli.[5] And so it is theorized that mirror neurons not only reflect the visible action of another person, they also reflect that which is not visible—the unconscious intentions and feelings of you and another person in a meaningful relationship.

This type of neural matching can be extrapolated to romantic relationships. In that way, neurons set up a mirror image of your partner's internal experience in your brain; simultaneously, mirror neurons connect your internal experience in your partner's brain (whether or not your partner's experiences are similar to yours or different). Reflecting your inner worlds back and forth, mirror neurons create a special link between you.

In an intimate relationship, each person mirrors the other's actions and feelings of attraction, romance, love, lust, and loyalty. To ensure that these heady experiences occur, mirror neurons trigger the release of love-inducing brain chemicals. For example, if your partner is feeling romantic, your mirror neurons connect to his romantic behavior, sensations, and feelings that prompt you to feel romantic toward your partner as well. When your brain releases chemicals, triggered by mirror neurons, your and your partner's mutual romantic feelings bring you both into a more intimate space with each other.

THE NEUROBIOLOGY OF LOVE

As we all know too well, relationship issues may result in resentment, disappointments, hurtful interactions, and a waning of passion. Your bright, shiny love of yesterday sometimes erodes so that your partner and you are instead connected in a dull, blighted bond: links of love transform into links of pain.

Here again, mirror neurons come into play in the erosion of relationships. A fascinating dynamic related to this is *projective identification*. Mirror neurons reflect hidden traits—those that we dislike in ourselves—that we have disconnected from our awareness and that remain in our unconscious. For example, if you hate your own anger, you may disconnect it in your conscious mind. In doing so, the anger becomes unconscious, and you act calmly. Unwittingly, in projective identification, you may act on that unconscious anger and provoke your partner to respond in an angry manner—that is, you project your anger onto your partner. With the help of mirror neurons, you will project your unconscious anger onto your partner, who will retaliate with anger of his or her own. In other words, your partner will identify with your hidden anger. The key to combatting the difficulties that arise from projective identification is to both gain insight into your feelings and find new healthy ways to communicate your feelings.

Projective identification is only one example of the many problematic relationship dynamics that you will learn about in this book. As long as both partners work, however, it is very possible to revise relationship dynamics. With earnest determination—on the part of both partners—to revive the relationship, mirror neurons can match up to help change painful links back to loving links.

To gain hope that we can change dynamics of pain to dynamics of love, that we can actually rewire the neural pathways in our brains, we will go back and understand how we got here, to where love fled and to how loving relationships became hurtful, and why it seems so hard to let go of the pain we incur in a relationship.

Remember when you first fell in love? Of course you do. Who doesn't? Falling in love is like walking on clouds, the headiest of experiences imaginable. We see the one we love as perched high up on a pedestal. Our mirror neurons trigger happiness, heartfelt wishes, and the hope that our lover will complete us and fulfill all our dreams for a happy life. The future stretches ahead before us, a shining path leading to the realization of our every desire. Those are the promises of a blissful, enduring love.

We owe part of this happy state of mind that love creates to nature. Love is essential to the survival of human beings; it is the greatest spur there is to that driving impulse of every living creature: procreation. And so nature has provided some powerful feel-great brain chemicals that act on our nervous systems and drive us to love. Sure enough, our remarkable mirror neurons not only connect lovers to each other but also recruit the other systems in the brain that support trust, romantic attraction, bonding, attachment, and lust—the components of love.

These systems work together to signal the release of certain chemicals. A cascade of those chemicals infuses lovers in a flash. Oxytocin and vasopressin—key ingredients for bonding and attachment—are released during sex, and they ensure trust, loyalty, devotion, and intimacy.[6,7,8] Testosterone and estrogen enter during romantic attraction and, of course, during sex.[9,10] Then there's dopamine, which plays a significant role in the pleasurable and rewarding states of love, romantic attraction, lust, and intimacy.[11,12] Norepinephrine also plays a role in the pleasure and reward circuits. To further heighten the euphoria of love and lust, the brain signals the release of endogenous opioid peptides (enkephalins, endorphins, and dynorphins) made in the brain, which are like morphine and nitric oxide.[13,14] Meanwhile, serotonin and gamma-aminobutyric acid (GABA) surge through the brain to fire up moods more than ever. Neurotransmitters, neurochemicals, and mirror neurons are riding high in the skies of love—and it all feels glorious.

But another reason it all feels so glorious is that love is blind. One of the most fascinating discoveries of neuroscience is that this isn't just a saying: our blinders actually have neural underpinnings. Caught up in the euphoria of love, our brains immediately get busy engineering a remarkable feat—they put to sleep the brain systems that trigger suspicion.[15] The very faculties our prehistoric ancestors developed to anticipate predators—wariness, doubt, skepticism, discrimination, and judgment—simply go dormant on us when we're in love. As a result, all we can see is our flawless lover and the untroubled future ahead of us.

Unfortunately, because of their chemical nature, our blinders wear off over time, and the future turns out to be somewhat troubled after all. In relationships, we argue, ignore, reject, betray, and disappoint each other. The areas of the brain that were asleep wake up, and distrust, depression, and anxiety set in. The damage, hurt, and altered brain chemistry fire our mirror neurons just as the good feelings did when love was in full bloom. We fail to realize our wishes for happiness and a lasting love. Our lover comes crashing down from the pedestal, and at the same time, we tumble from the clouds and land on the harsh ground of reality. Our neurotransmitters, brain chemicals, and mirror neurons take the painful fall with us.

As a result of our diminished brain chemistry and the loss of our blinders, we are left in a state of distrust and depression. When that state sets in, our mirror neurons trigger old wounds from our early years, light up sad scenes from the past, and connect us to emotionally heart-wrenching connections—times when we felt similar to how we feel during a loss of love. These associations—such as painful childhood patterns of relating or other painful relationships—climb on board our already-shaky love life, weakening it further and bringing more pain. The cumulative pain squeezes the life out of the relationship, and it feels like the end of love.

It needn't be the end of love, though. You don't want to put the blinders back on; once they're off, keep them off. But you do want to create a new relationship—an entirely new experience that can rewire and realign your mirror neurons and bring back the feel-good chemicals (for more on creating this new experience, see part 2). As you work your way through the new experience, your brain will slowly signal the return of serotonin, GABA, oxytocin, vasopressin, dopamine, testosterone, estrogen— those brain chemicals that ensure happy and calm moods, bonding, loyalty, lust, and ecstatic pleasure.

It takes only one person in a relationship to start the healing process, by creating a more solid self and a new, healthy dynamic. Once that person creates change, it's likely that the dynamic of the relationship will change (such as fewer negative feelings and behaviors, like hostility or despair). With continued work on the relationship, the other partner will also change in some ways. To picture how mirror neurons work, imagine that you own a bracelet of a linked chain. Move one link, and the adjacent link can't help but move also. Of course, if the bracelet is rusty, you may need to polish it up before the adjacent link will move. In a similar way, mirror neurons link you to your partner, so when you polish up, or begin to repair the relationship, if your partner is intent on polishing up the relationship, then he or she is likely to change also. Part of what contributes to the possibility of change is the phenomenon of neural plasticity.

OUR PLASTIC BRAINS

An exciting feature of the brain is its ability to adapt and to change, which is known as *neural plasticity*. Minds can change, brains can heal, and relationships can be repaired. We can change patterns of relating that in turn create changes in our neural networks.

Researchers have found that mirror neurons are endowed with the capacity to change.[16] Studies have also revealed that the same mirror neurons that link partners together connect to other brain cells that fire on multiple circuits, including those controlling motor action, nonverbal behavior, memory, emotions, and so forth. That means that when we change our behavior and feelings, our brains change as well, and we reflect those changes to our partner.

But change is not all that easy. And that is because old emotional, painful scenarios dig into the brain and impair change. Here is an example: For a woman in a relationship, no matter how hard her partner is trying to respond to her needs, because of her partner's past behavior, the woman's mirror neurons may not fire on his attentive and caring behavior. If he was previously wrapped up in his own world and neglected her, then old, painful feelings may come back to haunt her. The sadness, loneliness, and feelings of abandonment have taken root in her brain and color how she perceives his behavior in the present. It's those emotions of hurt that are so hard to let go of. Indeed, deep, lasting change does not occur instantly.

When we turn to the research, there is some promising news. The brain system known as the amygdala—the seat of the emotions that houses the fight-or-flight response to traumatic, painful events[17]—is also plastic. This finding suggests that emotionally charged memories, which have been linked to the amygdala, can change as well. That means that old traumatic and hurtful memories are not indelibly set into the brain or body: they can be moderated. But, as with all good things in life, doing so takes work and time.

The repair of prior flawed interactions and painful memories requires the will to change, patience, and positive new experiences. In this book, you will learn how to create fresh experiences for yourself and your partner. These fresh experiences can extricate old painful experiences and form new healthy experiences that modify your neural pathways.

Mirror neurons are at the heart of it all.

MONKEY BUSINESS: MIRROR NEURONS IN MONKEYS

Let's uncover these mirror neurons, central players in our love lives. They reside deep inside our brains and minds, and they've been there since our birth. Mirror neurons, however, were discovered only recently.

The mind-blowing discovery took place at Italy's University of Parma in the 1990s. Working with macaque monkeys, university neuroscientists discovered a grouping of tiny brain cells located in the premotor cortex, right behind the eye sockets. These cells, which were neurons, acted in a very particular way, one quite different from that of monkeys' motor and sensory neurons. The scientists called these newly discovered brain cells mirror neurons, because they found that the neurons acted like reflectors, mirroring the neuroscientists' unspoken intentions to the monkeys.

Ordinarily, when any individual, monkey or human, performs a meaningful action—reaches for a glass of water, for example—a group of neurons in the individual's system goes into action: motor neurons, visual neurons, auditory neurons, olfactory neurons. In other words, mirror neurons connect to all other brain circuits controlling movement, sight, hearing, and taste. In the Parma experiment, however, the scientists found that the monkey's mirror neurons were activated, or fired, when the monkey saw the experimenter performing an act. This firing of mirror neurons occurred not because of anything the monkey itself did but because of what the experimenter did. Simply put, when the experimenter reached for an object, a mirror image of the experimenter's action was recorded inside the monkey's brain. It was a process of neural matching that reflected the experimenter's actions in the monkey's brain—and thus linked the monkey to the experimenter.

But the discovery went even further. Rather than just having the monkey observe what the scientist was doing, the experimenters took it a step further.[18] An experimenter reached for an object, grasped it, and held it for one second while a monkey observed the actions. In this case, the monkey saw the entire sequence of actions; researchers referred to this as condition 1. In condition 2, the experimenter set up an opaque screen that hid his action. In this instance, the monkey saw the experimenter only reach for the object, not grasp or hold it.

What the researchers found was that the mirror neurons fired not only when the monkey saw the entire action but also when the monkey did not. In condition 2, the mirror neurons fired as if there were no screen, as if the monkey had seen the entire action. In fact, the monkey inferred that the experimenter would grasp or hold the object without even needing to see the entire action.

In this experiment, the mirror neurons acted somewhat like magnetic resonance imaging (MRI), revealing one individual's brain activity to another: they detected the internal motives of the experimenter, so that the monkey could anticipate the experimenter's intention and respond accordingly. It's as though the monkey were reading the experimenter's mind. The monkey "knew" exactly what the experimenter was up to, without having been "told" and having seen the experimenter do it. The Parma study thus showed that mirror neurons reflect not only seen action but also unseen action—internal motivations. The monkey and experimenter interpreted each other's internal states. That's the power of mirror neurons.

THE INSIDE TRACK: OUR OWN MIRROR NEURONS

You just saw how interfacing mirror neurons set up an interaction between monkeys and researchers based on interior states. Remarkable as the finding is, it doesn't show love. Not that monkeys don't fall in love; they do, but not in the same way that we do. When we fall in love, interconnecting mirror neurons reflect our emotions, empathy, attunement, intimate needs, and desires to our soul mates as they reflect theirs to us. That's what love—deep inside our human brains—is all about. It is this body of research—on mirror neurons and their connections to other brain systems—that I have drawn on in writing this book.

As you may faintly recall from Biology 101, neurons are brain cells that respond to stimuli and transmit information to the central or the peripheral nervous systems. The nervous system then processes the information and sends it on to the appropriate part of the body for action. Technological breakthroughs, such as functional magnetic resonance imaging (fMRI) and positron emission tomography (PET) scans, produce images of the brain as it functions and actually have made it possible to view these processes, much like a live video of our brain activity.

Using this technology, researchers have found an area of human brains that has mirror neurons.[19,20,21] Similar to the monkeys that inferred what the experimenter would do without seeing the entire action, humans do not have to see the entire action to infer what another person will do. In fact, our mirror neurons can respond to more than visual stimuli. Our mirror neurons give us the power to anticipate and respond to another person's intentions, which is the basis of meaningful interaction between two people. Mirror neurons link two people at a deeper, more intricate level than sight or sound do. How humans connect and respond to each other are functions not only of who we are but also of our complex internal wiring. In connecting us to intimate partners, every mirror neuron in each of us connects to between sixty thousand and a hundred thousand neurons in our brains and those of our partners; those mirror neurons in turn connect to an array of still more sensory and motor neurons. Imagine a vast, intricate system of approximately 100 billion neurons in our partner's brain connecting to 100 billion neurons in our own brain![22]

These connections are not arranged willy-nilly. Neurons are wired together in a complex system of circuits. When mirror neurons do their work, they stimulate other neural circuits, including those of brain chemicals, memory, emotions, viscera (or body centers), and motor centers (or action). But how can our brains tell the difference between a friendship and an intimate relationship?

In a fascinating fMRI study, researchers[23] identified the neural basis of romantic love and friendship. While volunteers who were truly, madly, deeply in love viewed pictures of their partners and friends, researchers scanned their brain activity. To measure feelings in the brain, the researchers looked at the areas that light up in the brain scans. They found that the brain scans of volunteers in love lit up twice as much in the areas that register love as the areas that register friendship. And for those in love, the brain scans that registered love and sexual arousal lit up twice as much for love as for sexual arousal.

The researchers also identified the areas of volunteers' brains that released oxytocin, vasopressin, and serotonin, which promote trust, attachment, and bonding. These same areas overlap with the brain's circuits that register pleasure and are rich in dopamine, norepinephrine, and endogenous opioid peptides. Moreover, the researchers found that, for volunteers in love, there was less activity in areas of the brain associated with distrust, anger, fear, and anxiety. When we fall in love, our guard comes down so that nothing gets in the way of our positive feelings: the brain activates love and pleasure circuits while simultaneously deactivating negative emotional circuits. So, the brain ensures that we fall deeply, madly in love.

Here's how intimate relationships play out: when partners interact, they each bring to the table their personality, their appearance, their attitudes, their moods of that day. But they also bring a lot of emotion, expectation, memory, history, culture, longing, and passion, which stay under the table and make the interaction intimate. Mirror neurons start playing footsie under the table, and because mirror neurons don't travel alone, they recruit other neural circuits to join them. It can get crowded under there.

We all have different backgrounds and come from different circumstances. Because of that, no two people experience the same reactions in their brain to something. For one person, a whiff of someone's cologne can trigger an emotional reaction of desire. The same scent can trigger a response of fear or revulsion in another person. It all depends on personal history, past experiences, culture, and individual temperament.

Along with our ongoing relationships and current moods, our early patterns of relating with others, which we first learn in family relationships, also influence our interactions with people in myriad ways. Maybe, because of an old relationship, we interact in a way that shows we are seeking attachment; or maybe our old response was to withdraw. Either way, our past interactions continue to influence how we interact with others.

Mood can also influence our interactions with others. A mood is the result of a process that goes on deep inside our brains. Chemical messengers, known as neurotransmitters, release good-mood chemicals in the brain. One of the chief good-mood chemicals is serotonin; another is GABA, which reduces anxiety. When people are depressed or anxious, their brains are not utilizing sufficient serotonin or GABA.

In fact, a new class of antidepressant drugs are known as selective serotonin reuptake inhibiters (SSRIs). SSRIs inhibit the sending neuron (the axon) from taking the serotonin it transmitted back into itself. The serotonin is able to stay around longer in the gap between neurons (the synapse) for the receiving neuron (the dendrite) to pick it up and then to interact with specific receptors in the brain.

When people are happy, relaxed, or in a good mood, the serotonin and GABA that connect to specific receptors flow. When we interact with others while in a good mood, our mirror neurons trigger the release of good-mood brain chemicals that stimulate happy feelings. Conversely, bad moods fire up the mirror neurons to connect to feelings of sadness.

We all have good days and bad days. On good days, our mirror neurons and neurotransmitters fire away. On bad days, when we are down, no matter the intensity of an interaction with another person, our mirror neurons no longer trigger the release of feel-good neurotransmitters. So our own personalities, backgrounds, patterns, and moods ground the responses of our neural and psychological systems. There's even more going on inside the brains of lovers.

TALKING WITHOUT SAYING A WORD: NONVERBAL COMMUNICATION

One of the ways that mirror neurons activate love-related brain circuits is through nonverbal communication— the communication, without words, of our unconscious needs, desires, intentions, and goals to another person. We all have used nonverbal communication: as infants, before we could speak, we connected to our mothers with body language, facial expressions, tone of voice, and eye contact. Adults still connect to others in these ways. For example, people often say one thing but mean something else, they may be unaware of their true feelings, or they may feel embarrassed about revealing them. How we talk (nonverbal communication) often speaks louder than words and reveals our innermost feelings.

Mirror neurons also have a role in nonverbal communication: in addition to connecting to emotional centers, mirror neurons connect to neurons that activate the visual, auditory, sensory, and other systems.[24,25] It is those connections that facilitate nonverbal communication. Thus, through mirror neurons, partners can nonverbally convey their despair, anger, or anxiety, as well as their hope, love, and intention.

EMPATHY, EMOTIONAL RESONANCE, AND INTIMACY

Some of the most important feelings in love are empathy, emotional resonance, and intimacy. When these aspects of love are degraded in a troubled relationship, mirror neurons have an important role in bringing them back.

Remember how the monkey inferred what the experimenter would do? We humans can also attribute meaning to others. For example, we may anticipate what someone else will do or think as though we were reading that person's mind.[26] Many couples in long-term relationships can finish each other's sentences. But empathy goes much beyond knowing what someone will do, reading your partner's mind, or finishing each other's sentences. Empathy happens when you resonate emotionally with your partner as your partner resonates emotionally with you. Putting yourself into someone else's place *emotionally* is empathy. Although empathy is an essential component of intimate relating, it is only one of many. Deep love requires emotional attunement, caring, romance, attraction, love, and lust.

Empathy doesn't just apply to those in love, but also to casual friends or even strangers. Wired with empathy from the get-go, we are born with the capacity to put ourselves in someone else's place.[27] Our innate ability to empathize with others helps us survive as a species. A striking instance of empathy took place in New York City on January 2, 2007. Wesley Autrey leaped off the edge of a subway platform and threw himself over the body of a man who had suffered a stroke. The man had fallen onto the tracks just as a subway train was pulling into the station at high speed. Autrey leapt down onto the man and placed his body tightly over him. The train was unable to stop in time and ran inches over his head. Then the train stopped a few inches later and they both survived. Indeed, Autry, known as the subway hero, saved the man's life.[28]

Because we are wired to feel and act out of empathy, our mirror neurons make it possible to experience what someone else is experiencing, and thus to be in sync with that person. In this case, Autrey's mirror neurons instantly connected to those of the stroke victim. Empathizing with the man's distress, Autrey went into action immediately. Autrey's well-oiled mirror neurons were partly responsible for his actions.[29]

In intimate relationships, things get more intense. Real intimacy is a deep, multilayered state of mind. Old patterns of relating trigger intense emotions that work their way through all those layers so that minds, old memories, and emotions unconsciously meet. Just how does this kind of empathy work? Again, it's important to remember that mirror neurons do not operate on their own. Instead, they connect to other neural circuits, including the limbic center, which is one of our emotional systems. So when mirror neurons fire, they connect with our body's emotional centers, thus laying the groundwork for empathy.

It's the emotional component, a kind of empathic attunement, that is the sine qua non of intimate relationships. It's why we cry when we watch a sad movie or salivate when we hear someone crunching into a chocolate chip cookie: we respond to those stimuli as if we ourselves were being stimulated. In these cases, when we are linked by mirror neurons, the barrier dissolves between ourselves and someone else. In a meaningful relationship, as your partner's mirror neurons fire, they trigger special brain chemicals, connections, and associations that flash across neural pathways in your brain, and vice versa.

Empathic attunement enables partners to imagine themselves in each other's place, to share in each other's internal experiences.[30] So if you feel sad but your partner feels angry, you can still experience his anger. And when he feels angry, he can still experience your sadness. Remarkably, when you feel sad, your partner's serotonin stops flowing and he can feel your sadness temporarily. For that moment, he can resonate with your feelings of sadness and you can resonate with his feelings of anger. You are emotionally attuned to each other, able to access each other's feelings, sensations, thoughts, needs, desires, and goals. What could be more intimate than emotionally charged empathic resonance?

Emotional connection is essential to intimate relationships, and it's at the heart of empathy, or the ability to be on the same wavelength as your partner. Research[31] has provided truly compelling evidence that we not only can get into other people's heads and understand them but also can *feel* for them. We can walk in their shoes; we can have empathy for them. In an intimate relationship, partners can experience each other's internal or unconscious lives and put themselves into their partner's shoes.

Clearly, empathy is a good thing—and for intimacy and love, it's a really good thing. But as with other good things, too much or too little empathy is not so good. The amount of empathy in a healthy relationship has to be just right.

♡ Too Much Empathy

Beth, a teary-eyed, lovely young mother of four children told me that she was no longer in love with her husband, Leon: "He doesn't pay attention to me. He's a workaholic, and that's all he thinks about." When I asked her how she confronted him with her hurt feelings, she said, "I don't confront him; I feel bad for him. I see that he's obsessed with work, but I understand just how he feels. I know how important financial success is to him. His friends all compare themselves to each other, so he's caught up in this competition. And he has to prove himself to his parents. I've lost myself in my kids and husband, so I don't know what I want. The only thing I know is that I'm no longer in love with Leon."

Beth has too much empathy for Leon. Yes, she walks in his shoes, but in doing so, she loses her own shoes. Healthy empathy means that you enter into your partner's inner world while at the same time holding on to your own inner world. Otherwise, like Beth, you lose yourself in your partner and end up feeling lonely, neglected, and invisible—and you lose the courage to speak your mind. This is not exactly the recipe for loving and being loved. The other side of the coin, of course, is not having the capacity for enough empathy, so that you are unable to step into your partner's shoes because you are too deeply entrenched in your own.

The One-Way Mirror

You may lose sight of your ability to empathize with your partner because of pain you're feeling yourself, or because of an old script from childhood that holds you back from empathic resonance and emotional attunement. When love goes awry, mirror neurons that once connected you in love to your partner now connect you to your own pain. In other words, mirror neurons misfire, and rather than reflecting your *partner's* inner world to you, your mirror neurons are reflecting *your own* inner world to you instead. In a sense, your mirror neurons act like a one-way mirror. Your brain no longer releases love-inducing chemicals or mood-enhancing neurotransmitters. Any previous energy spent resonating with your partner's emotional states now goes inward so you can attend to your own hurt.

When you love and are loved in return, mirror neurons act like two-way mirrors. You look into your partner's eyes to see the magic of love shining brightly, and your partner looks into your eyes to see the same. So the mirroring effect goes both ways But a one-way mirror blights empathic resonance and emotional attunement. The story of Mark and Amanda illustrates this one-way mirror.

The sun shone when Mark felt admiration and love; today, however, rejection cast its dark shadow on him. His desperate need for the world to love him occupied Mark from the time he woke up in the morning until he fell asleep at night. The love and admiration he hungered for consumed his attention, leaving him bereft of empathy for his wife, Amanda. He spent his waking hours trying to please others, at the expense of his relationship with Amanda. He was busy understanding others, but Mark didn't understand Amanda, and he couldn't begin to imagine why she no longer loved him.

Amanda felt frustration, anger, and pain. "I want you to understand me, to feel for me," she said to Mark. "You have no idea what I feel, what I'm really about. It's all surface stuff that you do to get others to love you. It's so you can be the big shot. It's always been about you." Mark's failure to empathize with Amanda, to be emotionally attuned to her, had simply eroded Amanda's love for him. He was great at superficial relationships with many people, but real intimacy escaped him, and he was unable to move past his own emotional needs to empathize with Amanda's.

His own emotional needs were substantial. Mark constantly needed approval, admiration, and love. Like an emotionally starved child, he went about looking to fill those needs with frantic energy, selling himself in every interaction. Mark was an expert at monitoring social cues so he could give people what they wanted. He spent enormous energy pleasing others so that they would take care of his emotional needs.

Why did Mark do this? He was playing out an old family script, one based on his mother's interactions with him. Married to an alcoholic, Mark's mother had experienced persistent mental anguish and was unable to emotionally attune to Mark. Rather than comfort him, she needed to be comforted. Rather than reflecting her son's needs, she required that he take care of hers. Rather than showing love to him, she needed him to show love to her. From early on, Mark learned how to please his mother so that she would love him. And that old script crept back into his adult behavior in his people-pleasing ways of relating.

Mark's behavior left Amanda feeling invisible,

unimportant, and taken for granted. Meanwhile, no one could fill Mark's emotional hunger, and he had managed to push away the one person who could really help him fulfill his needs.

But it was not too late for Mark and Amanda—they could still change things. Mark could learn how to bring Amanda closer again, and together they could bring love back. Mark could move from pleasing others in casual relationships to real, lasting intimacy with Amanda. In therapy, we harnessed Mark's social skills. We then applied his social skills to intimacy and to enhancing his nonverbal empathy, so he could emotionally attune to Amanda.

Nonverbal Empathy

A person's tone of voice, scent, posture, touch, eye contact, dilation of pupils, facial expression, and body language often convey emotional attunement and nonverbal empathy to other people. When these things happen during interactions, neural systems and mirror neurons trigger changes in our physical and emotional states. Think of it as a kind of social intelligence based on unarticulated sensory perceptions. Successful car salespeople, with their raw, keen insight, are a great example of this intelligence. They can size up customers in a way that most other people can't. They aren't psychic, but they truly connect with others. They can know what's going on inside a person before a word is spoken. Nonverbal communication—body language, tone of voice, timing, facial expressions—provide them with the clues to close the sale. With well-tuned mirror neurons, they are fully loaded with interpersonal social smarts.

Social smarts, of course, are not the same as intimacy. In an intimate relationship, being good at communicating nonverbally is particularly important. Knowing how to "read" your partner is an essential component of emotional attunement. Unfortunately, in our less-than-perfect world, there are times when mirror neurons go off-line and empathy breaks down.

Empathy Deficits

Not everyone is as well endowed with interpersonal social skills as people who sell cars, and few are as empathic as Wesley Autrey, who saved the stroke victim in the New York subway. For many people, family background, moods, and prior hurts can all lead to problems with social skills, attunement, and emotional resonance. We can think of these problems as garden-variety barriers to intimacy—they're not uncommon, especially among those who tend to have difficulties in social situations. But some people have another level of empathy deficit, a level considered extreme or atypical. And because mirror neurons facilitate empathy, people with extreme empathy deficits tend to have deficits in networks of mirror neurons too.

Autism and Asperger's syndrome entail impairments in social interactions and in nonverbal communications such as eye contact, facial expressions, body postures, and gestures. Deficits in emotional reciprocity and empathy go along with diagnoses. Sure enough, brain-imaging studies have revealed that people with autism spectrum disorders show evidence of dysfunction in their mirror neuron systems.[32,33]

Another example of empathy deficits is found in sociopaths and criminals, who can read others' nonverbal cues in ingenious ways. They often can understand just what someone is about to do and then manipulate the situation to their advantage. What the criminal mind lacks is the ability to empathize with others, with victims. Here again, studies have provided evidence for the link between a deficit in empathy and a deficit in networks of mirror neurons. Brain-imaging studies of criminals have revealed dysfunction in brain areas that connect emotions with mirror neurons.[34,35,36]

Such deficits are anomalies. What about the development of the average brain? Are mirror neurons there from the beginning? Are we really born to bond? To create lasting intimate relationships? The answer is an emphatic yes. As you'll see in the next chapter, infants show us how mirror neurons lay the groundwork for verbal communication, empathy, and emotional attunement from the get-go, helping develop our adult styles of relating almost from birth.

Chapter 2

Born to Bond, Wired for Love

Infant and Mother Links Live On

AT THE BEGINNING

Do you, like me, have an uncanny connection with one of your children? I often awaken with a promising feeling or even an ominous one about my son that I simply can't explain. Sure enough, when I do speak to him, my feelings are confirmed. What are these mysterious connections? Do we have these "psychic" abilities from the beginning? Indeed, we do.

Not only are we born to bond; bonding and learning begin in utero. These are the very attributes that are essential for the survival of our species. In fact, infant-mother attachment is a necessity. Because the period that human infants need to mature is the longest of all species, infants depend on their caregivers for quite some time.[37] During this extended period, infants' survival depends on close ties with the mother.

In one study, researchers studied pregnant women

during their last trimester.[38] The mothers read aloud *The Cat in the Hat* for a total of fifteen hours. Using technological advances, the researchers were able to track the babies' preferences. They found that after the babies were born, they preferred a tape recording of their mother reading *The Cat in the Hat* (which they had heard in utero) to a recording of another Dr. Seuss book, *The King, the Mice, and the Men*, which they had not heard in utero before.

Coincidentally, neural pathways are laid down during this vital stage of the infant-mother connection. Nonverbal communication activity occurs in the right brain, and so an infant's right brain links to that of his or her mother. Those links are critical for later interactions throughout life.

Recent studies with infants have suggested how, from the get-go, mirror neurons lay the groundwork for procedures like sucking, clinging to or avoiding the mother, and other forms of nonverbal communication. These behaviors and their feelings are the foundation for empathy, attunement, mutuality, empathic resonance, and reciprocity between mother and infant.[39,40,41,42]

To ensure infant-mother bonding and love, nature has provided endogenous endorphins and opioids.[43] As a result, bonding and love come naturally because they feel so wonderful. That blissful feeling in infancy is not too dissimilar from what we experience when we fall in love later in life. That ecstatic feeling—the one we want to re-create with our romantic partners and the one we hope will continue forever—is what binds us together in mad, crazy love. As a result, when love fades, debilitating despair sets in. A longing to revive that early ecstasy may well be the driving force for bringing intimacy back to a faded relationship.

Studies have shown that there is a close relationship between the neural underpinnings of maternal love and romantic love.[44,45] Mutual attunement, empathy, and resonance—which are vital to infancy and to the unique rapture of love—have a more commonplace but important function: they help regulate our physiological states. For example, when we feel blue, our facial expressions, posture, and body language tell that tale to others. If you feel down, you reflect your feelings to your partner, and he or she offers you a heartfelt hug into which you sink. The interaction not only can lift your mood but also can make your partner feel good about him- or herself. In a sense, this sharing of feeling states can help to regulate both of your moods. I have heard people speak of their partners as "making them feel good," and this remarkable phenomenon of mutual regulation is something that begins early in life.

Some renowned infant researchers have compiled three decades of amazing studies that delve into just how mutual attunement, empathy, and resonance regulate the internal states of infants and mothers.[46] The studies showed how, in a subtle feedback loop, infant and mother signaled each other with facial expressions, gestures, posture, and orientation, as well as the tone, timing, and rhythm of sound. The two were so attuned to each other that it was like watching a thermostat in motion. As each partner sensed emotional temperature changes in the other, the partners' mirror neurons fired almost simultaneously. When the process was disrupted, infants and mothers quickly reengaged in heightened emotional moments.[47] This precursor of intimate adult interactions is similar to the elation we feel when we make up after a fight with someone we love.

Let's take a peek at how the studies worked. Mothers and infants (between three and four months old) were seated face to face. Researchers used two unobtrusive video cameras, one pointed at the infant and the other at the mother, to produce a split-screen view of the interaction. The results showed that mothers and infants mirrored each other's facial expressions. Changes in their emotional expressions reflected their shared sensations, moods, and simultaneously released brain chemicals.[48,49,50] In an instant, change in one influenced change in the other; their matching mirror neuron systems were firing away.

Another finding of these studies was the matching of each person's rhythm. Infants and mothers each paused for a similar duration before the other took a turn in an action. For example, if the infant babbled or gazed at the mother, she waited her turn to babble or gaze back, and then the infant took his or her turn. This type of inter-action shows how closely attuned they were.[51] Through matching mirror neurons, infants and mothers created a shared dialogue defined by timing, but without words! This early rhythmic interaction lays the groundwork for interactions later in life. For example, we learn that in a healthy intimate relationship, one person does not talk over the other. Instead, partners take turns talking to create a rhythmic dialogue. Sometimes, a failure to create rhythmic dialogue can be damaging to relationships.

To Speak or Not to Speak

Darlene, a lean, long-legged, delicate woman, looked distressed as tears streamed down her face. Her husband, Bill, a rugged-looking man, had informed her that he no longer loved her.

"For the life of me I can't understand why, after twenty-one years of marriage, you suddenly want out. What's up? Do you have another woman? Am I no longer attractive?" Darlene fired off one question after another.

Clearly frustrated, Bill told me, "I've told her repeatedly why I was unhappy."

Seemingly oblivious to Bill, Darlene proceeded to reminisce about the good times, the romance, the magic, their vacations, their three children, their home, their friends, and so on, for a good fifteen minutes. Bill said nothing; he only nodded and wrung his hands.

I finally interrupted Darlene and turned to Bill: "Please explain to Darlene exactly what you are so unhappy about."

His response was not surprising: "I've been telling her over and over that I feel alone, that her head is somewhere else."

Wide-eyed shock and denial came from Darlene, as she vented her discontent: his lack of participation with the children, the house, the cooking, and the social arrangements. "I even have to initiate sex with you," she said. Darlene was the organizer, the actor, in the relationship, and Bill had simply reacted to her—until he told her that he was no longer in love with her. Bill began to speak about how he felt invisible and suffocated. Darlene continued to talk nonstop over him. This couple had failed to achieve a rhythmic dialogue.

Their experiences and personality styles played into this dynamic. When we discussed Darlene's background, she recalled her interaction with her anxious, emotionally unavailable mother, who lived in her own head and did not respond optimally to Darlene. While she was growing up, Darlene always felt unheard, invisible, and insignificant. Along the way, she has made sure that she has been heard and has felt important. In doing so, she inadvertently squelched communication with Bill and did not make room for him to respond to her optimally. Unwittingly, Darlene had re-created her original mother-infant interaction: she was overcompensating for her feelings of invisibility by playing the role of her inattentive mother. Incidentally, Bill was also feeling insignificant. In effect, mirror neurons were connecting them through their mutual feelings of unimportance.

When she recognized her pattern of relating as the root

of her problem, Darlene cringed. She explained that she had tried so hard not to follow in her mother's shoes. In doing so, Darlene chose the profession of medicine so that, unlike her mother, she could be independent and strong. What she failed to recognize was that her controlling, overbearing personality was not equal to strength. Instead, she was compensating for her feelings of insignificance and her fear of being like her mother.

When Bill met Darlene, he was thrilled that he had found his perfect partner—he felt that Darlene completed him. She filled in the gaps of silences that he, a shy man, abhorred. Their differences seemed to complement one another, until the differences stretched so far that Bill and Darlene became polarized. Bill, who was tall and taciturn, had grown smaller in stature and even more silent, while petite Darlene had become larger than life and more loquacious.

Bill talked with his own family to learn about his infancy so he could see how it had shaped his adult interactions. His mother had been an intrusive, overly cautious, worrisome woman who had hovered over him constantly. An outgoing, gregarious woman, she ran the show. Bill's father, a mild-mannered, quiet man, complied with Bill's mother. With a personality style resembling that of his father, Bill was losing himself in Darlene.

In therapy, we are all working on changing the dynamics of Bill and Darlene's relationship. Darlene is learning to listen to Bill and to have faith that it is safe to do so. Bill is learning to speak out without the fear of Darlene interrupting. As Darlene lets go of the reins, Bill is better able to find his free spirit. He is slowly becoming more assertive, and Darlene is more able to listen to his point of view and compromise.

In this snippet from Darlene and Bill's story, you can see how infants and mothers influence each other and how their relationship dynamics lay the foundation for later life. Their childhoods affected their relationship, but with mutual determination, they are reworking it.

Some couples try hard to fix their relationships, but they don't all necessarily make it. Problems in self-regulating or self-soothing link them in an ongoing tug-of-war that neither can win.

♡ The Jar and the Lid

Perfectly coiffed and suited, Kate conducted a white-glove inspection of the couch before she sat down. In contrast, Blair plopped down on the sofa and carelessly brushed long hair out of his eyes. The exacting lawyer and the artist, Kate and Blair found themselves in a not-so-stellar long-term relationship.

I asked, "Blair, does Kate worry about you?"

A boyish grin crinkled his eyes and he said, "Yeah, she does." The grin quickly turned to a grimace. "She's not only worried; she's suspicious of everything. I can't stand it."

"What do you do when you can't stand things?" I asked him.

Staring off into the distance, Blair responded, "I go into my studio and paint."

Kate's thoughts on his artwork were less sanguine: "It's not exactly his artwork that soothes him. Getting stoned on weed is more like it." She was getting down to business. "What the heck? I like it," he said. "It makes me feel good, at peace with the world."

Kate was not looking so blissful. She stiffened up and said, "I hate it. He's in his own world and I'm not part of it. I feel alone and abandoned. Like I don't count."

Blair defended his position: "I need the weed in order to create."

Kate shouted, "That's not all you need! What about the models?"

Nonchalantly, Blair turned the tables: "She's obsessed with the models. She imagines I'm having sex with them."

Kate stared him square in the face and spat out, "I'm not imagining. I know you're cheating. I came home early last week, and sure enough, your pants were unzipped. There's not just one. I checked your email. There's a 'Barbie baby,' a 'Svetlana sweetie,' and 'Lana, my love.' I printed out the emails. You're a disgusting pig."

White-washing Kate's accusations, Blair responded, "You're just paranoid." He tried to defend himself. "I fool around on email, maybe I flirt, but that's all there is to it. I can't stand these accusations. I'm leaving!" He stormed out.

Kate bowed her head, and tears streamed down her face. "I feel betrayed, humiliated, like a fool. I'm supposed to be this hot-shot lawyer who ferrets out the truth. I don't know how I didn't see that he was cheating. Why wouldn't I want to see the truth?"

I suggested, "For a lot of reasons, mainly when you want someone to love you, the truth hurts too much."

Kate struck out at me: "What truth? That he doesn't love me? Is that what you're getting at?"

Now I was in the hot seat. Blair reentered the room. "I don't love these other women; they mean nothing to me. You're the only one I love."

The other women did not mean anything to Blair, but they served a function. Unable to soothe his inner feelings of turmoil, Blair turned to substances outside of himself. Sex provided him with a similar fix; he could "feel good, at peace with the world."

After talking with Blair about his relationship with his mother, I could make some inferences from his recollections. A fearful, somewhat paranoid woman, his mother spent considerable time in her own head, where she was preoccupied with staving off imaginary danger. Attending to her son's emotional needs meant keeping him in her mind. Her mind, however, was too crowded.

An early memory of Blair's was revealing. As a nine-year-old, Blair got into a fight with a rough kid, who won. A broken jaw and two missing teeth later, Blair stumbled home. After scolding him and warning him that the next time the rough kid would break his bones, his mother began to cry uncontrollably, which foreclosed the possibility of her comforting Blair. As you can readily see, the failure in his mother's ability to soothe or regulate herself or her child had its roots early on. As a result, Blair had difficulty regulating his own emotional states. As time went on, he learned to compensate with drugs and sex.

Discussion of Kate's relationship with her mother told a similar tale. Kate's mother was married to a high-powered lawyer, and her mother's appearance and social calendar filled her mind. She adhered to the old credo that behind every successful man is a good woman. Kate's mother's unpredictable mood changes ranged from warm embraces to red-hot rages. At times, she hurled a glass of wine at Kate; other times, she set down the glass and held Kate in her arms. Magical moments alternated unexpectedly with hurtful fits of temper.

At an early age, Kate learned to anticipate her mother's moods. Getting out of the line of fire required constant vigilance. Even when her mother passed away, Kate took her everywhere with her: Kate's mother's unpredictable moods compromised a secure mother–child attachment, so as an adult, Kate had become overly vigilant and suspicious.

Every jar has a lid that fits it. Kate and Blair were just such a pair. Because Blair was unable to monitor himself, Kate obliged him. Blair's problems in self-soothing threatened to distance him from Kate, but she kept him glued to her through her surveillance skills. Despite their disparate patterns of relating, Kate and Blair were, at an internal, unconscious level, linked by their matching mirror neurons.

At an unconscious level, mirror neurons connect partners not only in similar traits but also in opposite traits. Despite her objections, Kate secretly envied Blair's carefree behavior, but that envy remained hidden in her unconscious mind. Mirror neurons connected Kate's unconscious mind to Blair's behavior, and so in a sense she lived vicariously through him by unconsciously deriving satisfaction from his cavalier behavior. In the same way, Blair's envy of Kate's meticulous behavior remained a hidden wish at an unconscious level in his mind. Mirror neurons connected his unconscious wishes to her behavior, and he lived vicariously through her. Unfortunately, this arrangement proved messy and hurtful.

In session, we unraveled this morass of painful feelings. Soon enough, Kate was able to recognize the role of suspicion and near paranoia in her interactions with Blair. Blair confessed and begged for forgiveness. He tried to repair the marriage by giving Kate whatever she wanted. His attempt at intimate dialogue wasn't quite enough. Listening to Kate's painful feelings only filled him with unbearable guilt. Kate's empathy went as far as understanding his internal world, but it stopped there. She wanted more empathy from him. Eventually, Kate asked Blair for a divorce. While every jar has a lid that fits, not every fit is airtight.

Indeed, like any endeavor, change and neural rewiring

takes hard work over time. Change can become a reality only if both partners want deep change. That means that the determination and willingness to work hard for deep change must be strong in both partners. In Blair's case, his idea of change was superficial and fleeting, so he left therapy. Kate has continued in therapy and today is a more secure, confident, and autonomous woman. If the relationship cannot be repaired, she will have the strength to move on. Although Kate and Blair failed to change their patterns and mirroring, many couples can succeed by applying the skills in this book.

INFANT-MOTHER ATTACHMENT

In the nineteenth and early twentieth centuries, Sigmund Freud talked about how childhood experiences influenced adult experiences. At the time, there were no brain scans or other sophisticated technologies to shed light on his theories. Today, however, things have changed. Modern technology has ushered in a new era of research pointing to how infant-mother attachments form the infrastructure that carries us through life.

Attachment styles, nonverbal communication, and regulation of moods are laid down in neural pathways during infancy, and we reactivate them in relationships throughout life.[52,53,54] Let me say a little more about the term *attachment styles*, which researchers coined in the 1960s.[55,56] There is a strong correlation between the attachment styles we establish in infancy through non-verbal mother-infant communication and those we use in our later romantic relationships. For example, if we were securely attached to our mothers as infants, we are more likely to feel securely attached in intimate adult relationships. If our attachment in infancy was more disorganized, anxious, or avoidant, we are more likely to find others to play out this interaction in our adult love lives.

In a study of depressed mothers, when the attachment process went awry, mutual regulation between mother and infant was disrupted.[57] Infants became preoccupied with self-comfort and regulating their distress. The infants turned away, embraced themselves, rocked themselves, and withdrew from interacting with their mothers. This study showed that problems continued on into adulthood.

Other infants monitored their caregivers excessively, and as adults, they became anxious, overly vigilant, or suspicious. Still other infants tried to get their mother's attention with distress calls, crying, and thrashing about. A mother's nurturing response and mirror neurons either kicked in or did not. The mother's ability to be in sync with her infant affected whether mutual regulation occurred.

As adults, we develop more sophisticated interactions than those we have as infants, but our neural pathways are laid down in infancy. Most of us would not thrash about when the man of our dreams looks away. We may, however, try to comfort ourselves, withdraw, or leave, or we may feel anxious and insecure and continue to try to get his attention. If he still does not respond, we're likely to up and find a new dream man.

The importance, then, of infant-mother attachments is the impact they have on our love lives as adults. The fact of the matter is that infants learn *how* to love their mother before they learn *why* they love her. They also learn how their mother loves them before they learn why she loves them. The *how* often precedes the *why* into adulthood. At an unconscious, neural level, our visceral responses often precede our conscious awareness. Our faces flush before we realize that we are humiliated, let alone why that is so. We hike up our shoulders before we realize we are stressed and much before we know the reason. So, cognitive knowledge does not necessarily regulate our bodily and emotional responses; our bodies give us away.

♡ The Importance of a Secure Attachment

Shortly after Claire was born, her mother was diagnosed with breast cancer. Her mother was left feeling depressed and preoccupied, so that she was not able to nurse her infant or gratify the infant's needs for comfort and security. With the infant-mother mirror neurons askew, Claire's start in life was far from optimal. But that was not all. Claire's father left the marriage and saw Claire only occasionally. When her mother was hospitalized for a mastectomy, Claire's grandmother cared for her. Her mother survived the operation, but sadly died a year later. Claire met with disappointment in trying to gratify her inner needs for secure attachment with her mother. Despite the love and devotion of her grandmother, Claire grew up feeling insecure, lonely, depressed, and clingy.

As an infant, Claire fussed and cried loudly when her needs were not met in a timely fashion. She would eventually withdraw, sob quietly, and try to soothe herself. Without a secure infant-mother attachment, self-soothing is nearly impossible. It is not that Claire grew up without any gratification of her needs, but she was always at the mercy of others to satisfy her. People found Claire most appealing, and so she received attention. That attention, from friends and casual acquaintances, quelled her inner pangs for real, loving attention. She never really learned how to reach out and fight for what she wanted. Her patterns of abandonment, disappointment, helplessness, and resignation were established in early childhood and lived on in her adulthood.

Lacking inner confidence, Claire did not pursue higher education and went on to do secretarial work in the local school district. There she met Dan, the school principal. It was love at first sight. Their mirror neurons reflected the glitter of attraction, romance, excitement, and lust to each other. Their courtship was filled not only with fun times and great sex but also with deep, meaningful conversations. Their love deepened and glowed. Dan promised to care for and love Claire forever, which was everything she ever wanted. She had found the perfect match.

True to his word, Dan loved, cared for, and was devoted

to Claire, who was finally happy—to a point. Her traumatic past had been stamped into her brain, and she reacted with anxiety and fear to anything that remotely reminded her of her childhood. No matter how happy she was with Dan, no matter how many times he told her that she was everything to him, that their love was forever, she still wanted more assurance. If he so much as glanced at an attractive woman—and invariably he did—she felt threatened that he would leave her. If he had to travel, she feared that he may not come back and begged him to stay home. If he hired a new secretary, Claire feared that he would find the new woman more attractive and leave. Her insecure attachment and her abandonment issues intruded on her relationship with Dan.

In turn, Dan resented Claire's clinging behavior and was growing impatient with her. The more she complained and pleaded for greater closeness, the more he dreaded coming home and the later at night he came home.

Claire is in therapy working on her insecurities and trying to build her self-esteem, a sense of competence, her independence, and her own interests. She has gone back to school to pursue a master's degree in social work, which she finds stimulating and satisfying. The feedback from her professors and her high marks help her feel more autonomous and valuable. As she creates inner change, her traumatized limbic system (which houses emotions) is beginning to recover. Learning how to help less fortunate people can be a fulfilling and great healing process.

As she grows and evolves inwardly, Claire is more able to feel secure and not as emotionally needy for Dan. Dan's desire to do his own thing occasionally still raises anxiety for Claire, but these days, she is better able to allay her fears. She has also developed new friendships, which help her feel more enriched.

Claire is working on creating fresh experiences, which helps her plastic brain reform and heal so she can recover from her traumatic early start in life. Dan is responding to her changes and actually misses her when she is not around. To Claire's surprise, he recently joined her in couples therapy. It is not as though Dan had no early family traumas that settled into his brain and behavior: he did, and he is working on them as well.

It is hopeful for Dan and Claire to know that as they change their inner worlds and interactions, their plastic brains are also changing. Their matching mirror neurons bring them in sync on their goals of reconnecting in new ways.

The Fixer and the Unfixable

"I don't feel as competent or as good as any of my friends." Laurie was trying to keep her tears at bay, and her face became tight.

"Doc, I don't know what she's talking about," John said, broad shoulders straining his jacket. "She's smart, she cooks well, she entertains, and she works part-time as a teacher."

"Big deal," Laurie said, grimacing. "My friend Marcia does so much more than I do. She's a lot smarter than me."

"But her kids are all messed up, on drugs, drinking, and can't even hold onto a job. Our kids are so successful," John responded. But his pride was one-sided; Laurie hardly looked a proud mother.

"That's because of you, not me," Laurie countered. "You did everything for our kids. I know I should be appreciative of you, but somehow I don't feel that way. I feel angry with you. How ungrateful and terrible of me!" Laurie cringed, blushing slightly.

"And why is that?" I pressed.

"I don't know," she said. "Maybe I'm not in love with him anymore."

John flashed: "You don't know what you're talking about. I love you, and I know you love me."

"I didn't say I didn't love you, but I'm not in love with you anymore." Her blush deepened as her body sank down into the chair. "I realize that I've been sick a lot, and you've taken care of me—and for that I'm so grateful."

"I did everything I could for you. The doctors said you should be in a hospital last time, but I kept you out of it."

After talking about family histories, Laurie arrived at a realization and said, "John reminds me of my mother. My mother also did everything for me, like John does."

"How does that make you feel?"

"I feel less able, less competent than other people. I'm afraid I'm slipping into depression again."

"Did you feel similar in your childhood?"

"When I look back, I always felt not as smart or as capable as other people. I guess I was always depressed."

"Is there any family history of depression?" I asked.

Laurie's slight body sunk. "My dad suffered from depressive episodes his entire life, and my mother got hysterical each time he broke down."

"How were they with you?" I asked.

"I guess Mom got hysterical with me. I was a burden to her, and I've been a burden to John over the years." She began to cry softly.

"You're not a burden. I can handle it," John declared loudly.

"Yeah, but you get angry with me," Laurie said through her tears.

"Well, I can't listen to how you keep putting yourself down and attacking me!" he bellowed.

"See how mean he is? Why can't you be kind to me?"

Shaking his head, John softened his voice: "I know I'm losing it, but I love you." His frustration was unmistakable.

Laurie said, "And I love you, but the passion is gone. Remember when we talked and made love all night? I don't think we can bring that love back."

"I do, and that's why we're here."

Laurie and John clearly had their differences, but their mirror neurons brought them together in mutual determination to work hard to rebuild their shaky marriage. Besides caring for each other and having a shared history—with children, grandchildren, a home, and friends—they were intent on working out their relationship problems.

And there were some serious problems that required hard work. Laurie had been beset with a lack of confidence and feelings of helplessness and dependency, whereas John oozed self-confidence, independence, power, and competence. His need to act as her powerful savior dovetailed with her need to be rescued. Their mirror neurons reflected their differences to each other. And the result was that their interactions were frustrating and distressing. As it turned out, the more John catered to Laurie and the more helpless she became, the more he looked after her and the less she believed in herself. Each time she plummeted into deep depression, his rescue fantasy kicked in and he tried, in vain, to save her. Unfortunately, he could not fix her.

Mirror neurons were at play here; they reflected John's strengths to Laurie and Laurie's need to John, who in turn wanted to be needed. If only they could have completed and enriched each other. Without help, however, they were unable to do so.

In healthy relationships, people grow from their differences, but in this troubled relationship, John and Laurie's differences became polarized—she grew more powerless, and he grew more powerful.

By delving into their childhood histories, we found the roots of some of the unhealthy interactions that were occurring in the marriage. Laurie's feelings of helplessness, dependency, and incompetence stemmed from her early infant-mother interactions. A sensitive, high-strung infant, Laurie was colicky and cranky. Her mother, a needy, anxious woman, would not allow her to cry even for one second. With interconnecting mirror neurons, Laurie's mother began to anticipate her infant's needs even before she cried. Laurie never learned to soothe herself, which left her without a sense of self-mastery. Growing up, Laurie had many friends, but she never felt she was as good as them. She always needed someone to look after her and shore up her confidence.

The roots of John's rescue fantasy were also planted in his early childhood experiences. Born to an overwhelmed mother, John learned how to care for himself early on. Busy tending to two young children—his brother, who was ten months old, and infant John—his mother found her resources stretched thin. Although she did not respond to her sons' needs immediately, when she did, it was glorious: mirror neurons linked them in loving, gentle caresses.

While growing up, John felt inferior to his brilliant older brother. As luck would have it, his successful, powerful brother was distant from the family. And so John could find his niche: compensating for his feelings of inferiority, he transformed himself into the good, strong, helpful son. He became the family fixer, which carried over into his other relationships. Laurie's vulnerability was appealing to him, and he thought he could act as her fixer, protector, and powerful savior. Unfortunately, Laurie was unfixable in his hands.

The couple embarked on a therapeutic journey. Their recovery was an example of neural plasticity at work. Their willingness to modify their behavior and bring positive new experiences to the relationship helped them rewire the neural pathways in their brains.

Insight into their respective childhoods has helped John and Laurie to be more compassionate toward each other. As John backs off from doting on Laurie and finds other interests, Laurie can take charge of herself more and more. In therapy, we have worked on ways that Laurie can build her confidence without John's directing her. That is not to say that he does not support her efforts, but he is learning to let her go it alone. She has enrolled in a doctoral program in nursing, and although the work is tough, she is sticking to it, while John takes some time off from attending to Laurie to play golf.

Their communication is beginning to look up, as they no longer talk about the doctors or the medication she takes for depression but about her day at school, his at work, and current events. They are working on forgiveness for hurts they have inflicted on each other. Love and lust are in the air, with promises of tenderness and passion.

— ♡ —

How a person feels and acts depends on his or her infancy and the modulations to the neural circuitry and mirror neurons in subsequent interactions. As the infant matures, his or her sense of a separate self develops, but the matching capacities of mirror neurons remain throughout one's lifetime.

In adulthood, our mirror neurons continue to fire involuntarily and instantaneously. We have no conscious awareness of the process. For the most part, when intimacy erodes, with the help of matching mirror neurons, we can work on relationship problems, bring healthy new experiences into relationships, rewire the neural pathways, and reconnect. When I say "for the most part," I mean that it takes hard work by both partners to get on the same page. Underlying the incentive for hard work is our basic human nature to attach, to bond, and to love.

Indeed, the essential human need for attachment and love is at the root of our ability to repair and reconnect. At an unconscious level, we all desire love. At a neural level, we are prewired to love. There is nothing quite like the promise of love. When things go awry, if we will it, our remarkable plastic brains have the ability to change.

Although it influences our present and future, the past, while a good place to understand and visit, is not a good place to live. Reliving the past only stamps the old, often traumatic patterns of behavior further into our neural circuits. The importance of new, positive, loving experience as a vehicle for change cannot be overemphasized.[58]

With our plastic brains, positive new experience can reorganize old neural pathways and change our unconscious ways of relating.

Part TWO

Rewiring the Brain, Repairing the Self, and Reviving the Relationship: An Inspirational Program

KEYS TO UNLOCKING THE BRAIN

Part of the difficulty in creating change in a relationship is that problematic interactions have become locked into the brain. The good news is that the brain is plastic, which means that you can unlock the brain, rewire it, and bring back fresh and loving interactions. To do so, you first must acquire the keys, or skills, to unlock the brain.

Among the skills you will learn in this part is how to recognize when old ghosts—childhood family relationships—are haunting you and encroaching on your current relationship. Rather than allowing the past to eclipse the present, you will learn how to see your partner for who he or she is and not for whom a particular parent or family member was in the past. You will then be one step closer to bringing back intimacy.

To create change in a relationship, you must also feel empowered. That means that you must delete the harmful societal messages and old family scripts that devalue independent, assertive, autonomous women. With this second key, you will learn three steps for developing a more confident, more vital sense of self and a satisfying loving relationship.

The third key is to communicate verbally and non-verbally, so that your partner can meet your needs. You can convey more positive and constructive messages—with nonverbal cues that match what you say—to restore greater intimacy to your relationship.

The fourth key addresses some essential skills required for intimate relating—the ability to elicit empathy, remorse, and forgiveness. Through simple exercises you will learn these skills, the very ones that go into hiding, when love goes awry.

Like a hall of mirrors—instantly reflecting the brains and minds of partners to each other—interfacing mirror neurons will link your partner and you in new, loving interactions. Brain chemicals will then bring about attraction, trust, devotion, love, and lust.

Chapter 3

Key #1: Visit the Past but Live in the Present

The first key to unlocking the brain from the pain of hurtful relationships is to address the old family patterns of relating. Once you recognize the role of those patterns of relating in exacerbating and even distorting your love life, you will be ready to disentangle yourself from them and focus on the relationship at hand.

Old family dynamics affect every interaction that you will address. Old family dynamics are the dramas of our early family lives—the less-than-optimal parenting styles or troubled sibling relationships that prompted our responses back then, the painful emotional experiences that we long ago relegated to our unconscious.

Just as our mirror neurons connect us to our intimate partner in the moment, they also connect us to these unconscious dramas from the past and harm our emotional and bodily connections. Here's what goes on deep inside the brain. When mirror neurons link intimate partners, every mirror neuron is connected to about one hundred thousand other neurons that, in turn, are connected to a vast system of one hundred billion neurons. In effect, unconscious old family dramas send mirror neurons scurrying to the areas of the brain that trigger sad memories, hurtful associations, and depressed and anxious moods. The brain then locks into these hurtful scripts by playing them out repeatedly in a relationship. By separating old family interactions from the current relationship, we make room for mirror neurons to link us to new positive interactions.

The first thing to identify is that an old family script is playing out and affecting how you view your partner and the relationship. How do you know that? One sign is that your reaction to your partner is over the top. The level of intensity—whether anger, anxiety, fear, sadness, or despair—is not commensurate with what is going on. Another sign may be that you are reacting differently than how you usually react to life's events. It may feel as though your partner is pulling on something deep inside of you from some other time and place. Chances are that your partner has tapped into a painful family scenario. Once you've realized that your reaction is rooted in the past, you can step back and say, "Here I go again."

For example, Claudia overreacted with fear and withdrawal from her partner Tony whenever he had a few too many drinks. What exacerbated her reaction to Tony was the old, painful interaction of a drunk, lecherous uncle and a terrified child who ran away and hid. Tony would then become furious. Once she recognized where her reaction was coming from, Claudia was able to see her partner for who he was (someone who did *not* treat her the same way that her uncle had) and welcome her partner's advances.

That's only one side of the interaction, of course. The other side involves the enraged reaction of Tony to Claudia's withdrawal. The culprit in this case was also an old family script: a depressed mother who was unable to satisfy the needs of young Tony. His efforts to get her attention were met with disdain. He recalled how angry he felt back then. Once he became aware of how the past was coloring the present, Tony could see that Claudia— unlike his mother—was not depressed and did not scorn him. Tony, then, felt freer to respond to Claudia in more attentive, loving ways.

Like unwelcome family members who barge in at the most inopportune times, childhood scripts can intrude in the present and bring back pain, slights, a sense of injury, disappointment, and resentment. To make matters worse, the release of serotonin and GABA, vasopressin, dopamine, endogenous opioids, estrogen, and testosterone—once triggered by mirror neurons—diminishes. Love-inducing and good-mood brain chemicals are in short supply during negative childhood situations, so when mirror neurons trigger those childhood scripts, they bring along the old moods, which exacerbates the current relationship. In a very real sense, the current relationship becomes a new stage on which the old scripts find fresh life. If we could just free ourselves from those painful family scenarios, solving problems in our relationships would be much easier.

Unfortunately, old interactions are not so easy to shed. Like old ghosts, they haunt us and impair our self-esteem, our communications, our emotions, and our capacity to empathize and forgive. Yet those are the very tools we need—a healthy sense of self, communication, feelings, empathy, forgiveness—if we are to resolve ongoing relationship problems. The solution? Rather than undertake the near-impossible task of getting rid of the ghosts, we must transform them into ancestors with whom we can live.[59,60] That, of course, is easier said than done.

Old family relationships are beyond our immediate awareness—they're in our unconscious—so we can't tackle them in broad daylight. It's difficult to swat at something you can't see, hear, or recognize. All too often, we repeat what's familiar, even if it's painful. No matter how toxic the old drama was, it's what we know. For many, constantly repeating the troubled past stems from an unconscious wish to finally right it. Over and over again, the old dynamics, playing out anew, intensify problems in a relationship. Meet Ellen, and you will see just what I am talking about.

A willowy woman, sixty-five-year-old Ellen was feeling the toll of age. And her husband, Lew, was not recognizing what Ellen wanted. She felt he simply did not "get her."

"It looks like I'm heading for divorce number three," Ellen told me.

"Do you really want a divorce?" I asked.

"No, I want to make this relationship work. But Lew is near impossible. We fight a lot," she said. "He's such a wimp. His kids push him around, his ex-wife bilks him for money, and he caters to his customers day and night. I try to be patient and explain that he's not really helping anyone and that no one appreciates him, but he doesn't listen. It's so frustrating."

"I see how angry you are," I said.

She replied, "You bet I am. I talk myself blue in the face, but he doesn't get it. Everyone comes ahead of me."

"That doesn't feel too good," I suggested.

"No, not at all."

"Does this sound familiar?" I asked.

"I guess so, sort of. Sergio, my second husband, had his music, his press, and his fame. It serves me right for marrying an artist with groupies who turned his head. I tried so hard to explain what was going on, that the attention was an ego trip, but he could care less. He needed his fans, not me. I'm just not lucky in love. Ryan, my first husband, who I thought was the love of my life, turned out to be a disaster. We met when at college and got high together—socially, that is. But I grew up and he didn't. I watched him slide into addiction, and try as I may, he ignored me. I yelled, fought with him, threatened to leave, but nothing worked. Ryan's drugs were more important than me."

"It seems to me that you want to feel special with a man, but they disappoint you."

"Well, Lew has been sweet in many ways, so he's not a complete disappointment. I told him he should come to couples therapy with me, and he said that he'd think about it."

"Perhaps while he's thinking about it, we could try to think about anything in your childhood that may be playing out in these relationships?"

In therapy, Ellen discovered that a number of childhood dramas were being repeated in her adult life. The relationship between her parents had been fraught with friction that stemmed from her father's drug problem. Fifteen years into the marriage, her father stopped doing drugs. Ellen attributed his sobriety to her mother's patience. Ellen was under the impression that her mother, an effective teacher, was responsible for restoring her father to health. The proof of her mother's effectiveness lay in his recovery.

If her mother could reform her father, Ellen was certain she could reform her spouses: that was part of her motivation to fix men. Like her mother, Ellen tried to reform her partners over and over. But why did her mirror neurons connect her to men who needed repair, who would not put her first? We did not have to go too far to see the attraction. At an unconscious level, these emotionally unavailable men reminded her of her father, who put drugs first. In some way, she kept trying to fix her father through these men.

Ellen's need to feel special was also borne out in her family dynamics. Her absent father, who worked hard and played hard, worshiped her younger brother, who was an all-star athlete. Her mother adored her older sister, who was beautiful and brainy. Ellen, the middle child, was agile enough, attractive enough, and smart enough, but her attributes paled beside those of her special siblings. In Ellen's mind, her mirror neurons were linking her parents and her siblings in special loving bonds, but Ellen felt empty, lonely, and insignificant. She longed desperately to fill her emptiness and loneliness, mainly with men. In her desperation, she overlooked red flags at the beginning of her relationships.

When Ellen saw how the old ghosts were haunting her and bringing back childhood hurts, disappointments, loneliness, and feelings of insignificance, she was better able to examine her relationship with Lew. She is now addressing her propensity to repeat the old dynamics: rather than trying to repair Lew, she is working on repairing herself. Surprisingly, as she refrains from lecturing Lew, he is more loving, cooperative, and attentive.

THE PAST AS PROLOGUE

What is uncanny about this repetitiveness is that your partner often resembles a parent or player from the past, as in Ellen's case. How often have you despaired that you married your father or your mother? Or cringed at the idea that you may be turning into one of your parents? It can be a shocking recognition to see your partner through a prism of the past—as one of your parents.

There's another twist to replaying these familiar dramas. If the new actor, your partner, does not resemble the old player from the past, you may unwittingly coerce your partner to enact the old script. That was the story with Gail and Nino.

Nino was everything Gail ever wanted—kind, considerate, caring—so unlike her overprotective, strict, restricting father. Yet ten years into the marriage, Gail complained bitterly that Nino was overprotective, controlling, and suffocating.

When Gail got into trouble for drinking while driving, Nino immediately came to her rescue. But a stern lecture followed the bailout. When Gail got lost in a dangerous neighborhood late at night, whom do you think she called? Nino, of course. Nino now insisted that Gail tell him in advance where she was going, with whom, and how she was getting there. Just like her overprotective, strict, controlling father, Nino wanted to watch over every move she made. The reason? Interconnecting mirror neurons made sure Gail's irresponsible behavior unwittingly coerced Nino into becoming like her father. And so Gail enacted an old script with a new partner, Nino, all over again—the rebellious adolescent defying her controlling parent.

The result was that Gail was a dismayed woman who had entirely lost hope in the relationship. "I don't love him anymore," she said. "The relationship is so hurtful and I don't see how the love can come back." But the truth was, for Gail and Nino, as for the actors in any relationship, the old scripts were not written in indelible ink. As you know by now, our adaptable brains let us rewire the mirror neurons, separate out the old dynamics, and replace them with new ones. And that's what Gail worked on in therapy. Once she recognized the old family relationship and how it affected her current one, she took steps to acknowledge her role in the relationship and to change her behavior.

At the age of forty-five, Gail finally left adolescence behind and joined the ranks of womanhood. As for Nino—with the help of reflections from his mirror neurons—he has changed and is beginning to trust Gail's emerging maturity. Two adults interacting in healthy ways have replaced an acting-out child and a protective parent.

Can you recognize the impact of old family dynamics and then separate them from your relationship? In this chapter, I will guide you to reach back into your childhood, to look as clearly and as objectively as possible at the interactions that, back then, fired your mirror neurons, brain chemicals, and neurotransmitters. And then we'll jump forward to see how the scripts you wrote in the past still affect your behavior today. Only by finding and identifying the old patterns of relating and hauling them out of your unconscious, where they've been hiding, can you be prepared to separate out the old interactions from the present. Then you can create change—internally and behaviorally. As you do so, you will interact with your partner in a healthier way, unfettered by the pain of your childhood.

Reliving old relationships can be an intense emotional experience, so don't be surprised to feel pain bubbling up to the surface. Welcome it if you can—whether you like it or not, it takes intense emotional experience to create change that is deep enough to be lasting. So dig deep enough to unlock the old dynamics from your brains and make room for your mirror neurons to connect to and reflect a new loving relationship.

In a sense, emotionally and mentally, you will become your own therapist. In the following exercises, you'll prod your memory so that, in essence, you take down the history of your childhood environment, your parents, your siblings, and the impact of your past on the present. The goal is to go layer by layer into the past to recognize your old family dramas. Once you see how old scripts are affecting your current love life, you'll be poised to untangle the problems and free yourself from them for a more loving relationship.

These exercises pose suggestions and questions that will help your recall, just as I do with my patients face to face. You should simply allow the emotions and memories

to come to the surface. That way, the old emotionally
charged dramas register more clearly; the clearer and more
vivid they become to you, the better you'll be able to guard
against their encroaching on your current relationship.
Once you consciously disentangle the old dynamics, you'll
be able to move a step closer to a new loving relationship. As you do so, your mirror neurons will trigger the
release of love-enhancing brain chemicals—like serotonin
and GABA—to bring back good times, happy memories,
intimacy, love, and lust.

This is a special time, and a private time. Ready? Let's
begin.

YOUR CHILDHOOD ENVIRONMENT

Every drama has a setting. The curtain rises or an image
appears on a movie screen, and the first thing we see is
an environment, which establishes us in a time and place.
That's why the first step in recalling your old family drama
is to imagine that you're creating a play based on your
childhood and building the set for the play. Go back in
your mind and recall the environment in which your family life played out, the backdrop against which the actors—
your family and you—played your roles in the old family
scripts. The following sections present various techniques
you can use to revisit your childhood environment.

Take a Tour of Your Childhood Home

Every member of a family has a different mental picture of their childhood home. Did you ever revisit a childhood home that seemed huge to you at the time, only to find that it was really just a small bungalow? If you had your own room, you may remember the home as spacious no matter its size. Or if you shared a room with one or more siblings, it may have seemed crowded to you. How do you feel, thinking about your childhood home? Can you trace any effects of your childhood home to your current relationship?

Now let's explore your past environment. Imagine yourself walking through your own childhood home and as you do so, get in touch with the old feelings, the dynamics of your family, and how they may be affecting your current relationship.

When Aileen, a patient of mine, took an imaginary tour of her childhood home, vivid memories arose. She recalled the crowded conditions—it was a walk-through flat that was home to seven children who were close to each other in age and in space. Aileen and her siblings were always in one another's hair and couldn't untangle themselves without rip-roaring fights. As an adult, Aileen bemoans the distance that separates her from her siblings. She wishes that she had closer relationships with them, yet she doesn't do anything about it. The heart of the matter is that the childhood living conditions continue to play out in Aileen's adulthood: mirror neurons misfire, and she feels as though she needs her space.

Sure enough, Aileen's husband, Bob, complains that Aileen is too distant. Proximity—their closeness and distance—has become a central issue in their relationship. Aileen needs more distance from Bob, and he, of course, wants to be closer to her. She has thrown herself into a demanding career that doesn't sit well with Bob, who feels insignificant. He complains that he misses Aileen and thinks she doesn't want intimacy.

After she got in touch with how the past was affecting her relationship, Aileen moved away from the past and moved closer to Bob. She now sees that, unlike her siblings, who fought one another for space and threatened one another's space constantly, Bob does not do those things. As she realizes that he does not crowd her or pose a threat, Aileen is beginning to embrace greater closeness with Bob.

Take a Memory Walk Outdoors

Once you've revisited the inside of your childhood home, step outside and take a memory walk. Let a place or moment outdoors recall a key childhood memory for you. Maybe the trigger is a location—a balcony, a backyard, a playground, the sidewalk, the inside of a car, a local stream, a campsite—any place that brings back memories of your family relationships.

Nadia's memory walk brought a poignant scene to her mind. She recalled a walk she took with her mother home from the hospital, where her father was recovering from a heart attack. Nadia had always felt she could never please her mother and that their relationship was strained and distant. But on that day, as they walked sadly and silently home from the hospital, things were different. For the first time, she was able to comfort her anguished mother, and for Nadia, she felt that she finally received her mother's approval. The resonating mirror neurons between Nadia and her mother triggered matching moods—at last mother and daughter were in sync. And Nadia repeated this pattern of behavior with her mother often, so it became entrenched in her brain. It is perhaps no wonder that, as an adult, Nadia became a social worker, a profession that empowers her to care for and comfort the weak and needy.

In her marriage, however, Nadia has reconstructed her childhood drama with a new actor, her husband, Sal. Sal, who is obese, has blood pressure and cholesterol levels that are over the top. Although he has survived two open-heart surgeries, Sal still doesn't take care of his health. Nadia constantly keeps after him to exercise, to eat right, to stop smoking, and to see his doctor. When he complains about his health, she comforts him, and matching mirror neurons link them in an intimate but unhealthy synchronism. Alas, the marriage has devolved into a relationship between a resistant patient and his persistent nurse. Sal feels bullied and nagged and wants out of the marriage. No amount of comforting helps. Nadia's childhood—and her recent comforting of her disturbed mother, whose approval and love she garnered—has intruded into the marriage as Nadia tries to comfort Sal. Of course, Sal is not her mother, and her ministrations do not meet with his approval and love.

Then there is the case of Eddie, whose memory walk took him to his backyard. Eddie's father was mowing the lawn, and seven-year-old Eddie ran in front of the lawn mower as he was chasing a ball. Even though Eddie crashed into the lawn mower and fell to the side, his father kept right on mowing straight ahead. When Eddie howled in pain, his father scolded him for behaving like a baby. The sharp pain of the blade and his father's rebuke still bring bitter tears to Eddie's eyes. It seemed that mowing the lawn meant more to his father than Eddie did.

In his relationship with Delia, Eddie has, in a sense, turned into his father. Oblivious to Delia's needs, too intent on getting his work done to stop and offer support, Eddie woefully neglects Delia—much as his father neglected him. Delia in turn feels the way Eddie did as a child: dismissed and insignificant. Eddie used the memory walk to come to terms with his past, and that put him on the road to a more loving relationship with Delia.

What about your own memory walk? Do you have a childhood memory that you see reflected in your relationship today?

Take a Picture of Your Parents

Every drama has its leading players. In your old childhood script, your father is probably the leading man and your mother the leading lady. Of course, if grandparents or other family members or caregivers raised you, they will be the lead actors in the scenario you recall; it's the people who brought you up who count. In taking a picture of that relationship, the accuracy of memory is not important. In fact, other people—your siblings, for example—may remember things differently. What's important is the way that *you* remember the relationship.

Some suggestions and questions follow to help you re-create a snapshot of your parents and retrieve old memories. If these don't trigger anything for you, go ahead and recall your parents in your own way.

What do you see in your mind's eye when you imagine your parents? Re-create a picture of what they looked like when you were a child. Were they tall, short, slim, stout, robust, frail? Freckled, pale, ruddy, wrinkled, or smooth skinned? Do you remember your father's hands as he read the newspaper or your mother's as she peeled potatoes? How about the sound of their voices or the clothes they always wore? What feelings bubble up in you as you picture the leading actors of your childhood script? Disappointment or delight? Anxiety, fears, frustration, and anger, or calmness and serenity? Loneliness or closeness to your parents? Sadness or happy memories?

Let's dig a little deeper to see who they were on the

inside. In your mind's eye, you'll look at their personalities and how they dealt with their own emotional lives. As you do so, tap into your own feelings.

Here I've listed ten sets of characteristics that are typically at play in parent-child relationships. Use the list as you try to describe your mother. Of course, these are just general characteristics, so feel free to use whatever associations you need to describe her. However you recall her, as you bring your mother's personality, moods, and emotions to mind, think about whether you see them in yourself. Do you see them in your partner?

1. Outgoing, social, and talkative, or introverted, reclusive, and quiet
2. Domineering or submissive
3. Cheerful, optimistic, and hopeful, or sad, negative, and cynical
4. Warm, loving, and demonstrative, or aloof, cold, and reserved
5. Trusting or suspicious
6. Frequently anxious and fearful, or calm and willing to take a risk
7. Kept her feelings to herself, but later exploded; or expressed her feelings openly in the moment
8. Emotionally stable and consistent, or emotionally unstable and unpredictable
9. Reacted to stress with equanimity, or responded with chaotic loss of self-control

10. Emotionally available and responsive, or preoccupied, depressed, and emotionally depriving to you

Now take stock of your father. Go back over the list, and apply the characteristics to him. Do you see yourself in either parent or in both of them? Do you see your partner in either parent? Attend to the feelings that bubble up to the surface.

♡ The Wild Child and Her Chaperone

Maria, like her mother, could be described as an emotional extravaganza. A highly extroverted, demonstrative woman, Maria's mother was preoccupied with her friends and social outings. Little, if any, attention was left for young Maria. In a desperate bid to get her mother's attention, Maria used to throw temper tantrums, stage hysterical crying fits, and pick fights. She wrote her script early on.

Maria later met Pierre, and they became the "perfect" match—that is, one that played out the old family scripts on a daily basis. As Maria saw it, Pierre didn't pay attention to her. When he did, he was controlling and paternalistic. For her part, to get the attention of her husband, a preoccupied, taciturn, and domineering man, Maria eschewed the temper tantrums she used as a child; instead, she spent wads of money, flirted outrageously, and threw her self-discipline to the wind.

When Pierre caught her in the act, he punished her by cutting off her credit cards and keeping her home—which is exactly what his father did to him. Prudence, austerity, and constraint were the tools Pierre's father used to escape his wife's extreme emotionality. Pierre learned how to use the same tools, enveloping himself in his schoolwork as a child to escape the noise and chaos of his mother's personality. As an adult, to escape Maria's extreme emotionality, Pierre still lost himself in his "schoolwork"; now that he was a college professor, he wrapped himself up 24/7 with his students and research. In so doing, he re-created his old childhood scripts with Maria. Their clashing old interactions were wreaking havoc in their love lives.

Once Maria saw how she had transferred to Pierre the family script of trying to get her mother's attention, she decided to disentangle herself from repeating the past. She is practicing self-discipline, spending less, and not flirting with other men in front of Pierre.

Pierre has become more attentive to Maria. In the past, Maria was not able to confront her impossible mother directly, and she expected the same response from Pierre. Now Maria has begun to confront Pierre by conveying her feelings of pain when he ignores her. In a sense, she has relinquished her role as the wild child, and, in turn, thanks to their interlocking mirror neurons that reflect the feelings of one partner to the other, Pierre has resigned from the paternalistic role of her chaperone.

Unfortunately, the way we interacted with our parents as children, even if long ago, can continue to affect the way we behave in our grown-up relationships. In a very real sense, our parents remain leading actors in our love lives.

Take Stock of Your Siblings

Now that you've seen how old scripts with your parents play out in your adult love life, let's look at how old scenarios with your siblings continue to have an impact. Siblings also play important roles in the old dynamics that we repeat in our intimate relationships. Of course, if you're an only child, this influence—and therefore these exercises—may not be as relevant, but you can still take a peek into the grief or joy you may be missing if you had siblings.

Either way, you're about to delve into questions for examining the relationships, forces, and processes that are typically at work among brothers and sisters. As with the exercise concerning your parents, examine the feelings that bubble up to the surface. You may be surprised to feel the intensity that this exercise provokes.

As you read the questions I pose in this chapter, buried childhood memories of your siblings will come to the surface—memories that are typically replete with uncomfortable feelings of jealousy, envy, anger, sadness, shame, or anxiety, as well as with more positive emotions of love, gratitude, joy, pride, or comfort.

I call these memories "sibling ghosts," for they can continue to haunt your intimate relationships in the present. Mirror neurons connect to memory neural circuits, bringing sibling ghosts forward and setting up a string of associated memories. In finding the ghost of a childhood interaction between your sibling and yourself, you may also recognize the role your parents played in that interaction, which can also point you toward the role you played back then and how that old dynamic affects all that you enact with your partner.

Cameron was a case in point. She recalled feeling insanely jealous of her beautiful sister, whom her mother favored. The script Cameron wrote went something like this: To garner her mother's favor, she studied like mad and earned high grades in school. But no matter what she did, she couldn't win her approval. Sure enough, today Cameron repeated this well-worn script by trying to prove her worth with her partner, Terrance, a successful lawyer. Although she worked part-time as paralegal, she also shopped for the best foods at the lowest prices, prepared gourmet meals, drove her children to numerous after-school activities, and constantly cleaned her house. Did she make the grade here any better than she did with her mother? Decidedly, she did not. Too worn out to have sex, Cameron had boxed Terrance into a spot where he wanted out of the relationship.

As she recognized the old dynamic that was hurting her relationship, Cameron was on the road to change. She had begun to take stock of her considerable strengths and to value herself for who she was and not for what she did. And she was not constantly testing her partner's love. As she continued to grow more confident, Terrance became more emotionally available.

See what I mean about separating out the old dynamics to forge a healthier you and a healthier relationship? As you go through the following sections on typical sibling interactions, allow your associated memories to rise to the surface and settle in your consciousness.

BIRTH-ORDER ISSUES

Where do you fit in the birth order, and what was going on with your parents when you were born? Maybe you're the younger of two siblings, and your parents were happily married when your older sibling was born, but contemplating divorce when you were born. Or perhaps you were the youngest child, and your father's business was in bankruptcy when you were born, but thriving when your older brother was a youngster.

Ann's parents were madly in love when she was born. Not yet married when she was born, they referred to Ann as their love child. Her father later went into the family business and felt financially secure, so he proposed marriage to her mother. Ecstatic, her mother accepted. She couldn't have been happier, and her mirror neurons matched those of Ann's, so mother and daughter reflected loving feelings to each other. Five years later, Ann's younger sister Sarah was born, only conditions had changed drastically. Her father's business had gone bankrupt, and he was severely depressed and angry. He displaced his anger and disappointment onto Ann's mother, whose world fell apart. A gentle, loving woman, she suffered in silence and, unwittingly, was unable to respond to Sarah's needs in an optimal manner.

Ann and Sarah's adult lives took different trajectories. Whereas Ann, whose needs were gratified as an infant, is happily married, Sarah, whose infancy lacked optimal responsiveness, is still single. Overly needy for love, Sarah pushes her potential partners away with her insatiable demands.

Ann and Sarah were born to the same parents—under different circumstances—and are leading quite disparate adult love lives. Does any of this sound familiar? Have you and your siblings led different lives influenced by events in your parents' lives?

COOPERATIVE OR COMPETITIVE?

Was your relationship with your siblings cooperative or competitive? Were all of you out for yourselves, or did you share with one another? If all went so well that sharing and cooperation were the order of the day, chances are that it's still that way today. If all didn't go so well, what script did you write back then? You may have learned the art of muscling in to get your emotional needs met, or of retreating and licking your wounds.

We have been talking about children's responses to family circumstances, but there is more to it than that. Born to the same parents, children come into the world with different temperaments and may well write different scripts.

Lila and Sherri are sisters whose basic natures affected their responses to family circumstances. Although their siblings were plentiful and the resources of their parents were not, the sisters' adaptations to the paucity of money, attention, and love differed.

Lila, the oldest of seven children, deprived of attention and optimal responsiveness, was born with a feisty, assertive nature. She shouted, threw temper tantrums, and eventually got her way. In school, she sat in the front row, shouted out the answers, and pushed her way to the front of the line. Fiercely competitive, she refused to share. She compensated for her early childhood deprivations by eating too much and competing with others. In her professional life, as an overweight, aggressive district attorney, she knew just how to throw her weight around to get everything she wanted, except a loving partner.

Sherri, the youngest, was born with a sensitive, shy nature. Whatever scarce time or energy her parents had for all the children, there were even fewer resources for Sherri. Bullied by her brother, Sherri did not have the gumption to fight back, and so she let others push her around.

Although passive in her friendships and her professional life, she was also cooperative. A bright, talented woman, Sherri excelled in school and in her career as a writer. Aware of her propensity to retreat, she hired a literary agent who did the promoting for her and was able to land her a lucrative book deal. In her love life, her partner was a controlling man, and although mirror neurons connected them in love and passion, she faced the fear of losing herself in him. They are in therapy now to rewire their neurons and revise their relationship. Are these or other old scripts playing out now in your life?

LOVING OR HOSTILE?

Was the relationship among siblings in your childhood home loving or hostile? What feelings did those relationships prompt in you? Trace how the old feelings triggered emotional scripts to see how mirror neurons are dumping them in the lap of your love life today.

If your childhood memory is one of loving sibling relationships, chances are that you bring love to your intimate relationship. How about hostility permeating your sibling relationships? Because we're all unique, the script you wrote back then may have followed any number of different story lines: fighting back ferociously, preempting hostility with attacks, caving in, or ducking the attacks. Do any of these ring a bell? Do they remind you of other responses? Be honest with yourself, and examine how these scripts affect your intimate relationship today.

Frank and Don are brothers who exemplify the scripts children may write during childhood. Strict disciplinary action by their punitive father resulted in the brothers' dissimilar responses and scripts. Frank, the older brother, rebelled against the rigid rules that brought his father's belt buckle smack down on his rear end. Growing up, he got into fights with tough kids, dabbled in drugs, and dropped out of school. His mother did love Frank deeply, even though she did not have the fortitude to interfere or to defend Frank. And so the script he wrote was to expect nothing from those who love you; life is tough and you have to fight for what you want. Today, Frank is a workaholic real estate developer going on his fourth divorce.

Don, the younger brother, avoided his father's harsh discipline. He assumed the role of the good, loving boy in the family to compensate for the bad-boy role of Frank. He recalls the sheen of his father's belt buckle that he learned to duck. How? By staying out of trouble. Often he secretly sided with his brother, but for fear of his father's wrath, he never stood up for Frank.

In Don's marriage to a woman whom he loves deeply, he also avoids any confrontation. When his children show disrespect to his wife, for fear of turning into his father, Don does not back her up. Don and his wife's thwarted love for each other brought them into therapy, where they've learned that matching mirror neurons help them move toward their mutual goal of readjusting their interactions, creating new patterns in their brains for a more loving relationship.

JEALOUS AND SUSPICIOUS, OR TRUSTING?

Were you jealous of your siblings or were they jealous of you? Was your relationship with them tinged with suspicion? Or was yours a family in which the siblings trusted one another openly and fully?

Stacy recalls being a daddy's little girl and learning early on how to get a man's attention. All the while, her brother Brett stood on the sidelines and seethed with jealousy. The man-trapping script Stacy wrote in the past is wreaking havoc in her marriage today. Stacy does not cheat on her husband, Neil, or even try to make him jealous, but—like Brett before him—Neil feels sidelined, and it makes him seethe with suspicion and jealousy.

Does any of this ring a bell? Do you suspect your partner of betrayal, or are you jealous of an alleged or real other woman or man? If you imagine or believe that your partner has a lover, trace back to see whether that suspicion is part of an old scenario based on a sibling relationship from childhood. Maybe it's time to give this old dynamic the heave-ho and right the problem in your relationship.

ENVIOUS OR GRATEFUL?

Let's look at envy, which is sometimes confused with jealousy. Jealousy plays out when someone is afraid of losing someone they love to another person. Envy, by contrast, is when one person badly wants what another person possesses. Jealousy usually involves a third person, whereas envy is between two people and their possessions or attributes. So, you can envy your friend's talents, material goods, or creativity, but if you worry that you'll lose your partner to another woman, you are jealous of her.

Were you or your siblings envious of each other? Dave's story is a good example. Dave's mother persistently played up his sober, studious personality in contrast to his sister Eve's cheerful, outgoing ways. She liked to talk about how suited Dave was to the world of physics and Eve to the world of socializing. Although it sounded as if she were praising both children equally, Dave envied his sister's upbeat personality and the fact that she was so good at attracting hordes of friends. Are you surprised to hear that he married a woman with the breezy, optimistic spirit of his sister Eve? Yet just today he called his wife a silly Pollyanna. That's envy.

In raising your family ghosts and welcoming them into your conscious mind, you're actually finding your way back to intimacy and love with your partner. Getting in touch with the dark feelings these memories evoke enables your mirror neurons to connect to your emotional childhood dramas. Indeed, old emotional scripts have a way of living on. Untangle those scripts from your relationship and go on a journey to self-realization. As you revise your role in the relationship and change your patterns of relating—with your plastic brain—you will begin the process of rewiring your brain by creating new neural pathways and circuits.

By changing the impact of the past on the present, with matching mirror neurons, you and your partner will be poised to bring love back and to experience your souls soaring. Love-inducing brain chemicals will help you on

your journey of bringing intimacy back into your relationship. The journey, however, takes a strong sense of self. In
the next chapter, we will work on creating a richer, fuller,
and more empowered woman.

Chapter 4

Key #2: Savor Your Strengths and Face Your Frailties

Imagine the glamour of a Belle Epoque Monaco casino, adorned with marble, bronze, and crystal. Visualize the supremacy, the strength, the shrewdness of one of the casino's top executives. Make a mental picture of what this person would look like. A man, right? In an industry that has always been dominated by men, Samantha is a powerful exception. With short black hair, broad shoulders, and curves in all the right places, Samantha, who worked in a managerial position in a casino, is all woman.

Today, however, Samantha was crying like a baby. Her shoulders slouched, she wrung her hands, and her sobs drowned out her words.

"Al's been coming home late at least two days per week. I think he's having an affair with his secretary. What if he leaves me for her? I don't know how I'd manage. Al makes a lot of money, and I've never had to worry about our finances."

I asked, "Don't you also make a good living?"

"Yes, I suppose I do, but I couldn't manage without him. He's so levelheaded and smart."

"Since when are you anything but levelheaded and smart?"

Samantha paused for a moment. "It's true at work that I'm brainy and efficient, but in my personal life, I feel stupid. I didn't even suspect anything was wrong, let alone that he was having an affair. She's probably young and hot, not like me. I'm over the hill."

"So, you feel inadequate. Perhaps you sell yourself short?"

"I guess you're right. I have so much confidence at work, but with Al, I have none."

Many women sell themselves short, even now in the twenty-first century. Like Samantha, they do not always savor their strengths. Why? Society has always shaped how women perceived themselves. The media bombards us with quick fixes and superficial, unhealthy messages. You can't turn on your television screen, boot up your computer, or open a magazine without sexy, anorexic young models jumping out at you. Botox, plastic surgery, and antiwrinkle creams promote the message that aging is not a natural process but a disease you can easily cure. What about women's strengths, such as assertion, independence, and autonomy? These aren't lauded but are denigrated—in sitcoms and in real life.

During Supreme Court Justice Sonia Sotomayor's confirmation hearings in the Senate, many people referred to her being "emotional." And she is a typical example of a high-powered, independent woman, who is *still* denigrated. Some women—particularly many young college students I see in my practice—feel inadequate, lack confidence, and depend on men to shore them up. That's not to say that women shouldn't depend on their partners for love and emotional, spiritual, and sexual fulfillment. It is when the pendulum swings too far and a woman loses sense of her self-worth that peril sets in. To compensate for those feelings of inadequacy and unworthiness, a woman may resort to unusual measures. Meet Darla, a woman who has done just that.

♡ The Dance of Dependency

Sobs racked her tiny body and Darla pleaded with me: "Please help me. I can't take this another minute. I…I…I… can't talk. I'm choking. My throat's closing."

"Can I get you a glass of water?"

Mental anguish had a way of choking Darla. "No, no!" she wailed. "Oh, OK, I'll have a sip." She haltingly began to explain: "Chuck was just diagnosed with prostate cancer. I'm so scared of being alone…I'm choking. I can't control myself. I want to die."

Deflating like a leaky tire, Darla sighed. Her eyes met mine. "Oh, boy, there I went again." Collecting herself, she continued more calmly, "I'm OK. Really, I'm OK."

The moment was short lived: "Let me tell you, I have no courage. I've always taken the easy way out." I was curious to hear about what Darla considered the easy way out.

Darla had used many escapes from her pain. Chuck was one of them.

"Chuck takes care of everything so I don't have to worry about anything," she said. "What would I do without him? He's very protective of me. Last night, I had a parent-teacher association meeting and it was raining, so Chuck wouldn't let me go. He was afraid I'd get into an accident." The corners of her mouth turned up slightly.

Sir Galahad does come in handy some of the time. It's nice to have someone to protect you from the rain, to not have to worry about anything—some of the time. But what's not so nice is feeling that you have lost your sense of mastery or confidence.

"Have you gotten into any driving accidents?" I asked.

"No, but I'm scared to drive in the rain, or at night, or on highways." Her anxiety was mounting.

"So you limit the scope of your activities?"

"Yes, I don't have the confidence to do things like that."

"In what other ways does your lack of confidence limit you?"

Darla responded with a smile: "I was offered this job to run a busy pediatrician's office. I love children, but…" Her voice and smile trailed off. "I was afraid it was over my head. Chuck knows all about the insurance companies I'd have to fight with. Who needs that?" What psychologist could disagree with her on that score!

"I remember you told me you wanted to be a pediatrician. What happened?"

"Yeah, I think I'd be a great pediatrician," she said, with a dazzling smile. "But it takes very high marks and years of studying. I didn't think I could do it." Darla quickly became a pouty little girl again.

"Chuck sheltered you from every storm, and now you're afraid you'll be left out in the cold?"

Darla began to take an escape: "I can't swallow. I'm choking. I'm falling apart." Darla fell apart to avoid looking at herself. Like taking drugs, gambling, and sexual promiscuity, losing control is a way to avoid self-examination.

"The idea of separation seems so scary that you're falling apart," I ventured.

"I'm weak, and I'm so ashamed of it," she said.

"You feel inadequate and shameful, but that doesn't mean you're weak," I offered.

Darla was not accepting my offer: "I am weak. When you went on vacation, I panicked and had a meltdown. It was hard. Chuck was away on business, so I clung to the children."

"You clung to the children like your mother clung to you." For a moment, I realized that I had failed in my empathic response to her—that instead of my mirror neurons connecting to her, they connected to her children due to my concern about them.

She looked startled. "What are you getting at? You don't know what you're talking about. My kids are fabulous. You should see Rita. She's so pretty. Everyone says she looks like me, with her curly blond hair and light blue eyes. She's a knockout, and everyone loves her. Adam is a jock and popular like me. I raised them right, if I say so myself."

The implication was that Darla was using her children to soothe herself and her own lack of confidence. For Darla, rage and fear soothed her sore spots, but they offered only temporary relief. In therapy, Darla agreed to look back to the relationships in her family to see if that could help her.

Darla's mother learned her style of parenting from her own mother, who was very overprotective. Feeling inadequate, grandmother, mother, and daughter believed that they could not fend for themselves. All three women had a man in their life who would "protect" them. Darla wanted to break that chain. When she saw that her feelings of inadequacy were rooted in that insecurity over generations, I assured her that she could learn new patterns and ways of relating that would change her neural circuits and her feelings.

Using other people' admiration, Darla sought to ward off her intense feelings of inadequacy and shame. But such bold desperation for admiration was alienating people. By following steps to rewire her old patterns in the brain and repair herself and her relationship, Darla began to feel more adequate, less needy, and more confident.

Stimulated by Darla's newfound strengths, Chuck now feels less burdened and is more in love with Darla than ever. Their matching mirror neurons are helping drive the resonance between them and their brain chemicals—serotonin, GABA, vasopressin, oxytocin, dopamine, opioids, and testosterone—and are fueling their love and sexual desire.

Strength comes in many shapes and sizes, male and female. To one person, strength means hanging in there through thick and thin, even if the relationship has deteriorated from magical love to ongoing misery. To another person, it means letting go, getting out, and starting over. For still another person, it means trying to get to the root of the problems and finding new solutions to restore intimacy. I bet all three of those options have crossed your mind at one time or another.

To bring back intimacy, it is essential to stop the brain from repeating the patterns of painful relationships. With a solid sense of self, you can step back, reflect, and recognize your role in problematic dynamics—but doing so isn't easy. That's because most people confuse a strong personality with a strong sense of self. Those with a strident, determined personality do not necessarily possess a solid sense of self. Scratch the tough-looking exterior, and you will come face-to-face with a fragile self at the core. There are a multitude of relationship issues, but two of the most prevalent ones are based on strong personalities that mask fragility. I call them the blame game and differences that divide.

THE BLAME GAME

Just how does strength manifest in a relationship? Does being strong mean that we stick to our guns when fighting with our partner? That we insist on being right? That we are rigid and unbending, and insist that our way is the right way? These things are about playing the blame game, and believe it or not, strength is the opposite of the blame game.

We've all played the blame game at some point. When couples habitually blame each other for problems, they can never resolve their confrontations, because both partners need to be right. Their matching mirror neurons trigger blame, attacks, and defense, and a wage a war that no one can win. Many patients tell me that their strong personalities are at work when they engage in a blame dynamic with their partners. But that's not so. At the center of the blame dynamic is a weak sense of self or poor self-esteem that is rooted in childhood. The patterns laid down in your neural pathways back then continue to propel that low self-esteem into adulthood.

To establish a strong sense of self in children, good parents climb on board with a child's moods, feelings, and thoughts. Mirror neurons and empathy are on track between parent and child, so that the child develops a strong sense of self—a true self. Emotionally unavailable, depressed, anxious, preoccupied, hostile, or controlling parents fall short in this stage of a child's brain development. A parent who insists that a child follow in his or her footsteps in terms of personality, aspirations, interests, or proclivities is not climbing on board with a child. Did your parents accept you as you truly were, or did they criticize and devalue you if you didn't conform to their views? The following paragraphs go over some scripts you may have written.

Perhaps in your wish to please and eagerness to conform, you lost your true self. Or maybe you rebelled, lost favor with your parent, and now feel unacceptable and unworthy. In either case, your self-esteem—built on an already shaky foundation—may be tenuous. In a fight with your current partner, you may defend yourself and blame and attack your partner. You may fight to be right, or you may give up quickly, sulk, and feel even more unaccepted or unworthy.

Those who have a strong sense of self are flexible and don't fear losing themselves when they take responsibility for their actions. In contrast, those with a fragile sense of self are rigid and unable to take responsibility. They defend themselves, attack, and bring out the worst in their partners. Heated blows further weaken a brittle sense of self in the blame game, where it's all about proving that you're right. When self-worth is contingent on being right, stomping on your partner's self-esteem is the name of the game. In this war of right and wrong, a weak sense of self becomes even weaker, and both partners wind up losing. What goes awry with partners who blame each other is that they don't know how they truly feel about themselves. Now meet Kristen and Lloyd, who have not faced their faults and are dueling it out in the painful game of blame.

♡ Unbending and Unloving

Lloyd loved Kristen, but Kristen didn't love Lloyd—that is, not anymore. Mirror neurons that once linked them in love now linked them in pain. Critical attacks, wound licking, and Band-Aids had marked their twenty-two-year relationship. The production of vasopressin and oxytocin, which promote trust and loyalty, was on hold. Rather than promoting pleasure in a loving interaction, their brains were producing dopamine and giving them a high from putting each other down.

Lloyd's narrow-minded, rigid personality was the reason for Kristen's attacks, and she blamed his hair-trigger temper for turning her off. His world was about being right—both at work and at home—and it cost him both his job and his loving marriage.

Lloyd built their home, did the cooking and the child care, and tried to make changes in his personality, but no matter what, Lloyd couldn't please Kristen—just as he couldn't please his father. Lloyd's weak sense of self stemmed from the old script that was laid down in his neural pathways during childhood. In a sense, by marrying Kristen, who was critical, Lloyd married his critical father.

Lloyd insisted that he and Kristen go to couples

therapy. Skeptical, Kristen believed that therapy was for weak, helpless people who couldn't figure things out for themselves. But weak and helpless she was. Raised by a critical, punitive single parent, Kristen's true self had been squashed. A false sense of always being right and dumping all the blame on her husband upheld her flimsy sense of self.

Blaming Lloyd for his rigidity, Kristen refused to recognize her own. She wouldn't give Lloyd any credit for the changes he made and continued to find more and more fault with him. Forgiveness is a mark of strength, but it was in short supply in Kristen's world. Lloyd's weak self-esteem spurred him on to keep defending himself, attacking Kristen, and holding on to a loveless relationship.

Kristen feared weakness and was determined to be a strong, self-sufficient woman. But despite their arrangement—she was the provider and Lloyd the caretaker—she lost respect for him and was pushing him away through her attacks.

Once Kristen realized how her need to feel independent and powerful was wrecking her relationship with Lloyd, she decided to continue in therapy. Kristen and Lloyd are now working to rewire their neural patterns, change their dynamics, and repair themselves.

Are you locked in the game of blame? How would you describe your self-esteem? If you're stuck in the blame game, your self-esteem probably doesn't let you truly value yourself deep inside. You can trace the old script that embedded the voice of your parents' criticism, inattention, or devaluation in your brain. Maybe you lost your true self by complying with or rebelling against that voice. Do you have a fragile sense of self-worth and wobbly self-esteem as a result? Either way, you need change.

DIFFERENCES THAT DIVIDE

Why do so many of us find someone we love, only to try to change him? Contrary to what you may think, trying to change someone else to be more like you is not a sign of strength. It is a sign of weakness, a way of not accepting your partner's differences.

When you have similar interests, beliefs, and values as those of your partner, mirror neuron networks transport you all the way up to cloud nine; but out of the blue, ominous forces can hurtle you down to earth with a thump. A clue to those forces lies in the blinders you surely wore during that first blush of love, which have fallen away to reveal clashing differences between your partner and you.

Although some differences can be divine, they can just as well be disastrous. Ideally, differences in personality traits are complementary strengths and opportunities for enrichment and growth. These types of differences can cement a relationship. Unfortunately, all too often, differences set up divisive barriers between partners. So how do you break down those barriers? The unproductive way to try breaking them down is by trying to change your partner so that he is more like you.

But there are problems with trying to change someone. You may think that dissolving any differences between you makes for ever-lasting love, but that is not so. For one thing, you can't manipulate someone else to change. Second, if you could transform your partner into a replica of yourself, you would then lose him as a separate person with whom you want to interact. Although fear of abandonment is often at the root of the problem of people who desperately need sameness, the outcome of living with a clone is just that— abandonment. Without your mirror neurons darting back and forth between you and your partner, you'd have no one to bounce off of, no one to comfort you, no one to stimulate you with fresh thoughts, insight, or emotions. That is the cost of striving for sameness at the expense of differences. Meet Ally and Mike, a couple whose mirror neurons have gone off track in their attempts to change each other.

♡ Beauty and the Banker

Mike walked in and quickly sat down at the far end of the love seat and crossed his arms across his body. His wife of five years, Ally, stretched out on the chaise lounge. Turning her head, she glanced at Mike: "He's so distant and unreachable. It's like I'm not there. He comes home from work and, without a word to me, plops himself down to watch the news on TV. He never talks to me."

Looking away, Mike said nothing.

Raising her voice, Ally said accusatively, "See what I mean? He doesn't answer." She was clearly frustrated.

Mike responded, "I work hard, and I'm tired and stressed when I come home from work. So I need to unwind."

Ally retorted, "I'm tired, too."

"What are you tired from? Playing with Billy?" he smirked.

"He doesn't appreciate what I do. Running after a two-year-old, cooking, cleaning, and shopping are not exactly easy. It's stressful, but I still want to talk with him."

"What's there to talk about? What Billy ate for breakfast, what stupid guy your friend Gail is dating this week?"

Ally winced but collected herself: "I like to talk about relationships, about decorating the house, but you're not interested. I want you to share my interests."

"You know nothing about what's going on in the world, not even about the economic crisis or our financial problems." Mike was not about to allow Ally to change him.

Neither was Ally about to let Mike change her: "He's so insulting, insinuating that I'm empty-headed."

"Well, you are empty-headed. Do you know what she watches all day? Cartoons with Billy and reality shows when he's asleep. Why can't she be more intellectually curious like me?"

"I'm not like you. Why can't you be more sensitive like me?"

Mike spat out: "You want to turn me into a potted plant. Well, no way."

"I can't stand his insults. He thinks I'm dumb and wants me to turn into a financial wizard. Mike, if you're so intellectually curious and smart, then how'd you get us into this mess?"

As his anger rose, the pitch of his voice rose an octave. "She's blaming me for the economic downfall. Not only does she blame me, but she wants to change me into a carbon copy of her. Where would we be if both of us were out in la-la-land?"

"That's so not true," Ally retorted indignantly.

"You conveniently showed no interest in our finances, and now that the house is in jeopardy for foreclosure, you blame me. Where were you all this time?"

Ally fired back: "Since you're a banker, I relied on you, which was a big mistake."

Disregarding her, Mike said: "She was a high-powered executive for a fashion magazine and made a lot of money. I've begged her to go back to work, but no."

"I want to take care of Billy; that's my job. If you paid more attention to him and to me, to my interests, my TV shows, to my friends, things would be different."

"Let me tell you something. If you showed interest in what I'm about, like watching the *News Hour* or reading the *Wall Street Journal* instead of watching soap operas and reading movie magazines, we'd have a better relationship. I want a partner in this marriage, but I don't have one. I'm alone."

Ally defended her position: "I'm alone, too. Where are

you when it comes to communication with me? You're in your own world, that's where."

In Ally and Mike's relationship, their differences were bringing out the worst in each other rather than the best. Fear of abandonment—based on old family scripts—was playing out in their relationship. And sure enough, both partners complained about feeling alone. Ally later revealed that she was adopted and that, although her adoptive parents were loving, caring, attentive, and affirming, at an unconscious level, she had always felt abandoned by her birth mother. The neural tracks of abandonment and fear of separation laid down during her infancy continued to affect Ally. Deep down in her unconscious, Ally had written a script that if she were good enough, loving enough, and pretty enough, her birth mother would not have given her away. This script encroached on her relationship with Mike. Her attempts to change him to be more like her were aimed at allaying her fears of separation.

Society also played a role in shaping Ally and Mike's views of each other. Ally was influenced by pop culture, which applauds young, beautiful moms. She strove for perfection in motherhood and in her appearance. Mike, however, a product of the 1980s, found his security in society's definition of a successful man—one with a beautiful wife, a child, a home, and a career.

In therapy, Ally and Mike are working to rewrite those old family and societal scripts and replace them with fresh ones. Rather than trying to change each other, they are trying to incorporate their differences—Ally is reading the newspaper daily, and Mike is reading children's stories with Billy. With interacting mirror neurons and renewed brain chemistry, Ally and Mike are beginning to experience greater intimacy. They are learning to rewire their neural patterns, repair themselves, and restore their relationship.

Before you can revise your relationship, you need to learn how to rewire your own neural patterns by strengthening the self. Like a flower garden that requires nurturance and care, your budding self requires the right care so that you can grow strong and flower. But before you plant the seeds, you must prepare the soil and then weed it so wild plants don't strangle new growth. In our day-to-day lives, those weeds can be the negative societal and cultural messages that preclude growth. Eliminating them is vital to self-empowerment.

As you begin to repair yourself and your relationship, you will free yourself from pernicious messages and constricting roles. You'll learn how to weed out the old childhood and cultural scripts and replace them with new scripts of intimacy and love. Differences, instead of dividing your partner and you, will enhance intimacy and create more excitement.

Your brain chemistry will get in the act, too—like water and sunshine, psychological and neurobiological changes will help you feel better. Once you create change within yourself, your partner's brain chemistry and mirror neurons cannot help but respond. Instead of a single species of flowers, your garden will be resplendent with contrasting colors, shapes, and scents, like the multiple facets of a loving relationship. The following sections present some exercises to help you build a stronger sense of self. The first task is to remove the weeds from your garden.

WEEDING YOUR GARDEN
Countering Insidious Societal Messages

We are all born and raised in a particular society that influences our sense of self. Many negative societal messages in our society can erode a solid foundation of self-esteem. To counter these influences, you will learn how to focus on your strengths while facing your faults. It is time to say good-bye to the old and lay down new neural pathways. In doing so, you can dislodge the old dynamics from your brain to make room for new ones.

The first order of business, then, is to weed out the disparaging societal messages about power or age, particularly for women. Allow your assets to surface so you can value yourself for who you really are—doing so is the basis of good self-esteem. This will position you to resist going back to old self-denigrating places.

A benefit of valuing yourself is that, when you do, your partner will begin to value you more as well. Likewise, when you value yourself, your own sense of self strengthens, and you feel better. In the process of valuing yourself, your brain releases more serotonin and GABA, which promote greater confidence and well-being. Thanks to mirror neurons, feelings can be contagious, so when you reflect those good feelings to your partner, he will resonate with them and reflect them back to you. Let's review the negative messages that you have internalized. The following are some specific persistent negative societal and childhood messages (hindrances) and ways to overcome them (resolutions).

THE HINDRANCE

You feel old and unappealing when you see young, beautiful models with smooth skin and long, shiny hair advertising anti-aging skin or hair products.

THE RESOLUTIONS

1. Reframe how you look at the situation. Tell yourself that, although you are probably twice her age, you also have twice her life experience, know-how, insight, and sensitivity.
2. Accept your limitations and create new vistas based on your strengths. For example, accept that your once-smooth visage is showing some signs of wrinkling. Remind yourself that these signs of aging add to the charm of savvy, sexy women.
3. Savor the strengths of age, such as knowing that you have survived life stressors and have grown more resilient to be able to face new challenges.

4. Think about what your needs and desires are—maybe you want more leisure time, creative activity, spiritual awareness, or a more passionate love life. By facing your faults and mental blocks, you use positive messages to arrive at better place and meet your needs and desires.

5. Recognize your accomplishments at home and at work, and embrace the effort that you put into your achievements. For example, at home, you may know just how to support your family members without dictating or neglecting their needs. At work, you may have picked just the right moment to ask for a raise.

THE HINDRANCE

You compare your body with the bodies of skinny twenty-something women at the gym, and you always fall short.

THE RESOLUTIONS

1. Change how you view yourself by taking stock of your strengths. There's much more to you than the surface. Appreciate your body, inner beauty, and depth.

2. Join a gym or exercise program to firm up your body. The endorphins you release during exercise will make you feel better, and you'll like the results.

You are more than twenty pounds overweight.

THE RESOLUTION

1. Begin the process of weight loss with a sensible nutritional diet and exercise. At stake are not only your appearance and confidence but also your personal health. Good health will afford you more energy and greater satisfaction in your love life and career.

THE HINDRANCE

You are comfortable being in control at work, but you feel that you have to dumb yourself down when you are with your partner.

THE RESOLUTIONS

1. If you are happy in your career or in a powerful position, relish your accomplishment. Doing so will help build your self-esteem.

2. Recognize that the roles that our society has foisted on women are now outdated. It is time to free yourself from those shackles.

3. Value your own strengths, and then your partner will be able to value you too.

4. Focus on dualities. Accept that you can be both strong and soft, tough and tender. Only then can your partner and you cherish each other as fuller, richer people.

The plasticity of your brain will help you create new patterns, and in doing so, you'll be able to reclaim your strengths and renounce negative societal messages. And with the help of mirror neurons, you and your partner can reflect those changes to each other. The result will be greater intimacy.

WEEDING YOUR GARDEN SOME MORE
Deleting Damaging Childhood Messages

THE HINDRANCE

Your parents did not recognize or validate your real strengths and had other expectations. When you reflect on the scripts you wrote back then, you hear your parents' critical, punitive, or demoralizing voices.

THE RESOLUTION

1. Counter those voices and replace them with ones of approval. Rewrite the message "I'm not good enough" to "It was a difficult situation, and I did the best I could do at the time." This will help you focus on your assets and bolster your self-esteem.

THE HINDRANCE

You did not meet your family's expectations and have made mistakes along the way.

1. Cherish the freedom you gained by living authentically. If you took risks or fell on your face a few times, you no doubt gained valuable experience from those adventures and have grown stronger as a result. Take heart in knowing that plunging right into life and love is much more fulfilling than living life on the fringes.

2. Look on the bright side: the upside of taking risks is that, at the end of the day, you will not bemoan any lost opportunities.

THE HINDRANCE

You complied with your family's expectations and lost your true self. You now experience your life as constrained and meaningless, and you feel that you are a prisoner to other people's expectations.

THE RESOLUTIONS

1. Now is the time to free yourself and begin the journey of life your way. The battle for a freer, more meaningful self is not an easy one, but when you finally win, you can't help but cherish your strengths.

2. Imagine what you can engage in now that you formerly thought was too risky, and then do it! If you always wanted to play an instrument, sing, or dance, but never took lessons for fear of not being good enough, then sign up for lessons.

3. Challenge your inhibitions and follow the music and movement. You can get into the groove in a Zumba or dance class at the gym. That such fun activity provides you with a feeling of exhilaration is a result of the brain's release of endogenous opioids and dopamine.

THE HINDRANCE

You feel self-conscious and worry about how you look to other people, so you refrain from trying new things.

THE RESOLUTION

1. Free yourself from the chains of self-consciousness. At this point in your life, you should feel free to do things your way and have fun doing them. The only way you will know if you like something is to try it. Your greater autonomy and independence will create new patterns in your brain so that you will reflect a more adventurous, invigorated person to your partner. Mirror neurons and dopamine will work together to connect your partner to your exciting new self—he won't be able to help being fascinated by you.

THE HINDRANCE

You have difficulties with separation—you may have suffered an early loss in the family or have been separated from your parents in childhood. Or you may have felt

abandoned by your parents and now have separation issues.
The script you wrote during childhood may continue so
that, as an adult, you cling to, control, or suffocate your
partner. In turn, your partner pulls away and, in essence,
abandons you.

THE RESOLUTION

1. Pull back from your partner. Rather than feeling
   abandoned, discover how your independence helps
   you feel secure and more powerful. Indeed, it takes
   strength to control your inner world, and in doing
   so, you'll be changing your relationship dynamic as
   well. In the process, mirror neurons that link you
   and your partner will help you feel more comfortable
   and closer.

THE HINDRANCE

You avoid intimacy in a relationship: this is your attempt
to defend yourself from the pain of your partner's possibly
abandoning you. Many single people protect themselves
from intimacy by engaging in multiple relationships at
the same time. They don't get too close to any one person
so that there are always others to mitigate any hurt. Or,
maybe, your relationship has become one of friendship,
routines, or devotion, without passion or lust. If that is
the case, it may be a sign that you are avoiding intimacy.

1. Face your fear of intimacy. Recognize that is it is an old script that you can rewrite in your plastic brain.
2. Change how you relate to your partner so that you can achieve a fulfilling relationship—one with love, caring, and nurturing, along with passion and lovemaking.
3. Reach out to your partner to initiate lovemaking. When you bring love and lust together, you will bring back intimacy. (See chapter 9 for more on connecting love and lust.)

THE HINDRANCE

You precipitously leave a relationship to avoid having your partner leave you first. Is this a pattern you recognize? You may yell out, "I've had it!" or even threaten divorce or breakup during fights. In these cases, the fear of abandonment may be rearing its head.

THE RESOLUTION

1. Change this dynamic with your partner by staying present, working on discord, and resolving problems to forge a more fulfilling intimate relationship. Cowards often flee, but courageous people work on their issues and rectify them. Doing so will help build your self-esteem and strength.

Your parents coddled and overprotected you, and now you feel inadequate and dependent on someone else to take care of you.

THE RESOLUTIONS

1. The best medicine is to challenge how you view yourself. Take stock of your strengths—warmth, friendliness, kindness, and inner beauty.

2. Making decisions on your own is one way to feel independent and enhance your self-esteem. If you don't feel confident making a decision alone, instead of leaning on your partner, try researching the answer on your own—even on Google. You can make an informed decision, which will feel empowering.

3. Feel more autonomous and powerful by charting some new directions. For example, if you aspired to a certain goal but didn't undertake it for fear of failure, go for it now. Take a course or join a group to hone your skills. The water may be choppy at first, but as you master your strokes, you won't be able to help feeling stronger and exhilarated!

THE HINDRANCE

You fear surrendering to your own inner feelings and to your partner. As a result, you develop a rigid, constricted personality and miss out on the vitality of life and the ecstasy of lovemaking. At root is a weak sense of self that is not firmly planted, the result of possible emotional neglect by parents. The specter of surrender is fraught with the fear of losing yourself.

THE RESOLUTIONS

1. Surrender to yourself—your inner fears, needs, desires—and see what bubbles up. It may be overwhelming. Even if it is, stay in the moment, and experience the feelings of helplessness.

2. Have faith that your plastic brain can be retrained and that you can untangle yourself from the morass of emotions to remobilize yourself. You can always pull yourself together. Instead of avoidance or denial, strength entails working through issues in your emotional life. This exercise of surrender and recovery will only enhance your sense of self.

3. Once you know that you can surrender to your deepest demons and come out of the experience stronger, surrender some of your responsibilities to your partner, let him take over, and allow yourself to rely on him.

4. Surrender yourself to your partner in lovemaking so that you find yourself again. Enjoy the rush of dopamine as you experience the thrill and ecstasy of erotic passion and power that arise.

– ♡ –

The preceding suggestions may or may not resonate with exactly how you experience societal messages and childhood scripts that hold sway and have shaped you. We all have different histories and cultural influences. If the ones that I have mentioned here do not strike a familiar chord, get in touch with the singular influences that have shaped you. Once you have looked at your strengths, faced your frailties, and weeded your garden of harmful influences, you will be ready to plant the seeds of strength for fullblown, empowered womanhood.

PLANTING THE SEEDS OF STRENGTH
Step 1: Visualization

Use your imagination to visualize a powerful woman—in the media, politics, literature, art, or business, or in your circle of friends and family—and try to identify with her strengths. We all admire different attributes in women, so your choice should reflect your unique proclivities.

Your idea of power may reside in your grandmother, who baked up a storm and recounted colorful stories, or from your mother's uncanny intuition. Or you may choose a writer like Toni Morrison; a powerful mother and politician like Hillary Clinton; or a soft-spoken, tough-minded anchorwoman like Katie Couric. Visualize the strength that you admire developing in you.

You may admire traits like tenderness, toughness, softness, stridency, cooperation, or competitiveness, or you may resonate with traits like intellect, street smarts, or other forms of brain power. Then again, you may admire talent for musical instruments, voice, dance, painting, sculpture, cooking, communicating, or socializing. These suggestions may or may not resonate with your likings. In the event that they do not, then visualize exactly what you admire in a woman. Then imagine in detail your more empowered self out in the world and at home.

Now visualize a couple you know or have seen interacting in a loving manner, a couple for whom getting along is more important than being right, for whom differences bring harmony and not acrimony. Chances are that the woman's self-esteem can allow her to handle being wrong and to value differences. Imagine that your self-esteem can be strong enough to accept these attitudes too. Research shows that the plastic brain can actually begin to change itself when you use your imagination.

Step 2: Modeling

You have cleared away some roadblocks and have visualized a woman with a firmly planted sense of self. Now model the behavior of that woman, who values her strengths and can face her frailties. The following are some observations about self-confident women:

- They feel good about what they know and are willing to learn more and continue to grow. Try modeling those attitudes.

- They communicate by listening and taking turns in a dialogue. If you tend to talk over someone or get lost in someone else's conversation, think of the woman you admire and model how she communicates.
- They value themselves by caring for their minds and bodies. Indeed, self-care is an integral part of developing a strong sense of self. With that in mind, join a gym; dance with your friends in aerobics class; and focus on nutrition, diet, and physical health. A healthy body goes hand in hand with a healthy mind.
- They show pride in themselves through pulled-back shoulders and a head held high. Try those on for yourself, and most important, do not forget to smile. If you smile at someone, he or she will smile back at you. And when you respect and love yourself, others will respect and love you.

One of the substantial benefits from following these strategies to rewire your brain and repair yourself is the effect that doing so has on your relationship. Your partner—linked to you through mirror neurons—cannot help but feel more attracted to you and more stimulated by your emerging strengths. Brain chemicals like serotonin and GABA, which enhance good moods, along with dopamine, oxytocin, vasopressin, and testosterone, promote loving, lustful feelings that flow more freely. Once you feel better about yourself, you are on the way to replacing the old hurtful relationship that was locked into your brain with a fresh, intimate one. Although you have not arrived at the Garden of Eden yet, it is not far off.

Chapter 5

Key #3: Communicating Needs
The Words and the Melody

♡ The Words: Verbal Communication

Alicia had a narrow face and a narrow-minded attitude. Her idea of a relationship was one that was strictly on her terms. Paul merely caved in to her. Alicia dominated, and Paul submitted, and that arrangement seemed to work for them. That she hurled insults at him and he simply caught them seemed to work for them. That she professed to have all the answers and that he had none seemed to work for them. All of those things seemed to work for them on the surface. Dig a little deeper, though, and we find what did not work for them—mirror neurons were connecting this couple on a one-way street in Alicia's direction. It was always what, when, and how Alicia wanted things.

True to form, Alicia, who claimed to have her finger on the pulse of the relationship, pointed to the problem. The difficulty in their relationship, as she saw it, lay in their inability to communicate. That was part of it. The other part, which was unspoken, involved their sex lives.

In their early forties, Alicia and Paul had not made love for the past two years. It was not that they fought, it was not that they did not care for each other, it was not that they did not love each other in some way—it was something more intangible. What exactly was it?

"He's like my two-year-old daughter; he doesn't listen. When I talk, he's not there," explained Alicia.

Paul looked off in the distance and said nothing.

Exasperated, Alicia bellowed, "See what I mean? He doesn't say a word. He has the personality of a wet noodle."

A blank stare accompanied Paul's nonchalant reply: "What should I say?"

"You're still obsessing about my affair with Stan."

Sheepishly, Paul uttered, "Well, yeah, it bothers me. I love you, and I thought we had a good marriage."

I asked, "Paul, do you think that not having sex for two years is a sign of a good marriage?"

"She's not into affection or sex, so I thought I would wait."

I asked, "Do you miss sex?"

"Of course. I love affection and sex, but we have everything else. I guess, though, that she's getting something from him that she doesn't get from me."

Alicia responded, "You're right, Stan's manly, and he stands up to me. You wimp away, so I don't respect you. We don't know how to communicate." She didn't mince words.

Paul assured me, "It's OK. She's upset, and she really doesn't mean it."

"I see how hard it is for you to confront Alicia," I noted.

"I don't like to confront anyone," he said softly. "I don't like to fight."

"What's so bad about fighting? At least I communicate. You don't. You're like a weak woman," Alicia said.

This, then, was the root of their problem. Alicia's style of communicating entailed confrontation, whereas Paul abhorred a fight and avoided confrontation; for Alicia, however, confrontation meant clearing the air. The more he backed away, the more she pursued him by badgering, bullying, insulting, and intimidating. The more he felt intimidated, the more he disappeared into himself. The more she acted aggressively, the more passive he became.

It is not as though Paul's assertion or testosterone were in short supply, but he did manage to mask them. When he found out about Alicia's affair, he secretly enlisted her family to stop her. Rather than confronting her straight on, he called her parents behind her back: he betrayed her much as she betrayed him.

Needless to say, Paul's passive-aggressive behavior enraged Alicia even more—so much more that she shifted the blame from herself to Paul, all because Paul did not want to speak up for fear of a fight! Neither Alicia nor Paul knew how to communicate in a way for the other to meet individual needs.

Paul desperately needed Alicia's respect, approval,

affection, and love—none of which he got. In turn, Alicia wanted Paul to show strength, decisiveness, and action. Above all, for her to be sexually attracted to him, she needed him to "be a man."

In therapy, Paul is learning to address issues head-on instead of in a passive-aggressive way or behind Alicia's back. Although confrontation is not the norm for Paul, he is beginning to feel safer and more comfortable in his relationship. His tone of voice, gestures, body language, and posture match his more forceful, forthright, decisive, and assertive words. In turn, Alicia's verbal and nonverbal communication conveys tenderness, acceptance, and respect.

The more Paul is present, the more Alicia is turned on to him, and she is less critical and more affectionate and loving. With more pleasant communication between them, romance and lovemaking are a stronger possibility. Alicia feels more mellow and feminine now that Paul is showing more masculine strength in communicating with her.

When love and lust fall by the wayside—as in Alicia and Paul's case, or maybe in your own case—so does communication. The reverse holds true also, so that when communication goes, so do love and lust. Matching mirror neurons are off track, and brain chemistry is diminished, so you and your partner don't really connect at an emotionally and sexually attuned level.

The left hemisphere of the brain is the home of language, linear thinking, and cognitive functioning. To get your needs met, you need to learn how to use words that

your partner can hear and respond to. You can replace off-putting statements like "You never get it right" with statements that describe your own feelings, like "I feel hurt." In other words, instead of pointing your finger at your partner, you can turn it inward. Only by communicating in this way can your mirror neurons and those of your partner line up to trigger the love- and lust-enhancing brain chemicals needed for intimate connections. Here's how to do it.

communicating Needs Verbally

1. Listen to what your partner says without interrupting or defending yourself. Remember that you are not in a court of law, and your partner is not an adversarial attorney.

2. When your partner has finished, paraphrase what he has said. Then ask if that is what he meant.

3. If you do not understand, let your partner explain something further. Do not defend or attack him; simply listen.

4. Paraphrase once more to be sure that you understand. When your partner agrees that you understand him, it is your turn to respond.

5. Go back to the first step, but now it is your turn to talk. Your partner will listen and paraphrase until he gets it right.

6. Take turns in these exercises and try hard to listen, paraphrase, and communicate your needs and desires by using "I" statements and not defending yourself or attacking or insulting your partner.

7. Make a pact with your partner to stop each other if you inadvertently say hurtful things. You may employ a hand signal or say, "Not fair."

As you continue, you will begin to understand where your partner is coming from, and your partner will get a handle on where you are coming from. That is the first stage of getting your partner to meet your needs using words to bring back intimacy.

THE MELODY: NONVERBAL COMMUNICATION

As we all know, a love song requires not only words but also a melody. In many cases, you may forget the exact words to the song, but the melody sticks in your mind. In the previous section, we worked on the words—on verbal communication, which resides in the left hemisphere of the brain. Now we'll work on the melody—nonverbal communication, which resides in the right hemisphere of the brain. It's through nonverbal communication that partners "sing" of their unconscious associations, feelings, sensations, and emotions.

The right hemisphere is where our earliest scripts were originally written, and then laid down by matching mirror neurons in infancy before we could talk. To expand a relationship through emotional resonance and to create deeper layers of change in the mirror neurons, communication from right brain to right brain is a must. The road to emotional resonance is nonverbal communication.

It's often not what we say but how we say it that counts. And that takes us back to the basics. How often have you laid eyes on a child and known how he or she felt even though there were no words spoken? You may have felt psychic. Maternal abilities boil down to reading the child's nonverbal cues. Red faced, tears streaming down his or her cheeks, head bowed—with nary a word, you get the picture.

It's another story when it comes to your partner, when hurt has turned your attentions away. By turning inward to heal yourself, you obscure your ability to read your partner's internal world. Your nonverbal reading skills go off track, and mirror neurons link your partner and you in miscommunication and pain.

We all want our partners to be "into" us, to attune to us in an intimate way. You and partner can practice some exercises—in which you both take turns—to achieve this closeness. As you do the exercises, your partner will begin to see you in his mind, and you will begin to see your partner in your mind—a perfect reflecting pool of interacting mirror neurons and intimate lovers. As both of you take turns in the exercises, in effect, you practice three key aspects of a loving relationship—equality, mutuality, and reciprocity.

Much like the previous verbal communication exercises in which you and your partner took turns listening and paraphrasing until you got it right, these exercises also entail taking turns. The difference is that now you will track nonverbal cues and verbalize them until you get them right.

The research on cognitive behavioral therapy—an effective and popular school of behavior-based therapy—reveals that your behavior determines your feelings, not the other way around. Scientific evidence of this can be found in the work of the psychologist Paul Ekman, who researched facial expressions.[61] His studies revealed that voluntary facial actions (someone intentionally re-creating a facial expression to display a specific emotion) generate changes in people's autonomic and central nervous systems and are specifically related to their emotions. For example, in our case, if you ask your partner to model a behavior, he will then associate that behavior with his feelings. In other words, his actions will elicit his emotions or feelings.

The idea here is akin to the game of charades, but with a twist. In charades, someone acts out a word or phrase without speaking, and the other players try to guess that word or phrase. In nonverbal communication exercises, you instruct your partner to act out a feeling or emotion, and he gets in touch with the feelings that his actions brings to his mind. You then guess what he is feeling. For example, if you ask your partner to stop making eye contact (for the purpose of the exercise), he takes on whatever emotion he associates with lack of eye contact, and then you try to determine what those underlying emotions are.

In real life, your partner may have difficulty describing his feelings in words, but if you can read his behavior or nonverbal cues, you will feel closer to him. The purpose of these exercises is to enhance communication for greater intimacy.

These exercises are only a guide for you to learn how to recognize various nonverbal cues. You and your partner may communicate actions and feeling in other ways that are unique to the two of you—and if that's the case, you should apply those ways here. The exercises here don't cover all the possible types of nonverbal communication that may arise in real conversations between you and your partner. Think of them as helping you heighten your sensitivity to various types of nonverbal cues. Once you get the idea, you can apply the exercises to real-life conversations. In the end, you'll be listening to not only the words but also the melody.

Exercises

Go through each of the seven main methods of verbal communication discussed on page 127, and apply them to nonverbal communication and cues, along with some possible meanings nonverbal cues convey. Ask your partner to model the cues and to really get in touch with what they mean to him emotionally but not share that with you. According to cognitive behavioral research, modeling a behavior will generate feelings. You can then guess which feelings the behavior evokes for him. I have listed some possible meanings or feelings that he may be experiencing, but you can come up with others of your own. For example, maybe your partner stops using eye contact when he feels guilty, or maybe he stops using eye contact when he's bored.

Tone of Voice

Try to block out the content and focus instead on the feelings your partner is conveying with his tone of voice.

He speaks softly and unsteadily.

- He feels sad.
- He feels lonely.
- He feels shame.

He speaks in a shrill, loud, or harsh voice.

- He is conveying hostile feelings.
- He is outraged with you.

- He is deflecting his inner pain with angry outbursts.
- He's just angry, and you have nothing to do with it.

Body Language and Posture

He stiffens his body with his arms folded tightly across his body.
- He feels anxious or uncomfortable.
- He feels angry.
- He has his guard up and does not trust you.

He hikes up his shoulders.
- He feels annoyed with you.
- He is an uptight person.
- He wants things his way.

He clenches his fists and leans forward.
- He is hostile.
- He's thinking of kissing and making up.
- He feels angry.
- He is trying to make his point by getting in your face.

Putting It All Together

Now that you've practiced reading each other's nonverbal cues by focusing on one feature at a time, you are ready to put it all together for the whole picture.

He speaks softly and tightens his facial expression.

- He is trying to be conciliatory, but he feels anxious.
- He is disingenuous and does not mean what he is saying.
- He's conveying mixed messages.

He suddenly cuts you off, turns his body away from you, and speaks coldly.

- He feels hurt and is trying to protect himself from you.
- He fears confrontation and so is avoiding you.
- He is furious.

He gives you a come-hither look, addresses you huskily, and leans forward with his arms outstretched.

- He wants to make love with you.
- A good fight brings out the lust in him.
- He totally adores you.
- His seductive overtures are aimed to get you to forget his negative behavior.

At this point, you are both on the road to a better understanding of each other, which will help bring you into a closer, more attuned relationship. Through your mirror neurons, your partner and you can begin to connect at a deeper emotional level. You may begin to feel that you "get" each other—an emotional resonance that is the essence of real intimacy. With matching mirror neurons, this emotional resonance is communicated by what partners say to each other but also, more importantly, by how

they say it. It is in the how—nonverbal communication—
that we convey emotions. And our mirror neurons connect
to emotional centers and to the central nervous system,
which facilitates nonverbal communication.

In these exercises, you employed nonverbal communication. The exercises charged your mirror neurons to bring
new, positive experience into the relationship. It is that
very experience that will continue to rewire the brain on
the road to intimacy.

To get a better idea of how this process plays out, meet
Charlene and Ray, whose nonverbal communication was
louder than words. Before Charlene and Ray learned
about verbal and nonverbal communication, they sort of
listened to the words, but they certainly did not hear the
melody. In the end, they were working to listen to both.

When Actions Speak Louder Than Words

Ray smiled and said, "My wife's so lovely. I don't know
what got into her. What does she want from me?" He
peered at me over his glasses.

His wife, Charlene, was shrieking at the top of her
lungs. "You must be kidding. What's with the little-boy
innocence? You know exactly what I'm talking about. It's
your terrible temper."

"That's not true. I'm not angry with you," Ray professed.

Throwing her hands up in the air, Charlene protested
loudly, "Oh yeah? Who are you kidding? You're furious

that I work. You heap insult after insult on the people I work with, on what I do, on the hours I keep, on everything except the money I bring in. It's not my fault you got laid off."

Ray stared at Charlene but said nothing.

Charlene met his silent rage with rancor. She bolted upright and said, "I know we're in an economic crisis. But I didn't lose my job. Wanna know why? It's because I keep my cool, and I'm in control. Not like you. You're out of control."

"I'm neither angry nor out of control," he said, striving to be calm. He glared at her intensely, and clenched his fists.

Charlene pulled away from Ray.

Ray became enraged and shouted even louder: "She doesn't communicate with me! She does this all the time. How can I communicate with her when she shuts me out?"

I gave Ray and Charlene a copy of the verbal and nonverbal communication exercises to work on at home. In the next session, they informed me that the exercises were helpful and that they had inspired other scenarios and feelings.

Charlene told Ray that his nonverbal cues confirmed for her how furious he was with her. "It's that scary look in your eyes, how you glare at me, how you're hot under the collar, how your fists clench and your body stiffens. As for your innocent, little-boy grin, that seems fake and manipulative."

"See what I mean? She's smart, all right, but she's

impossible. Her shrill voice is anything but cool and under control. I can't take this anymore." Ray pounded the couch cushion and lurched forward. Charlene's body froze and she stopped dead in her tracks—then she started to cry.

I asked Ray to look at Charlene's nonverbal cues and tell her what he saw. He insisted that she was dismissing him, that she didn't care about him and that she only cared about her work.

Charlene, still unable to face Ray, said, "He's way off. I'm not dismissing him; I'm afraid of him, and he scares me."

I encouraged Ray and Charlene to examine any old family ghosts that might be affecting their relationship. Ray got in touch with his feelings of humiliation, insignificance, and ineptitude. When Ray was a child, his father was critical and demanding. Ray recalled how his father dismissed him because he "didn't know what he was doing" and how his father said, "You're so stupid." Ray's family script was playing out in the relationship with Charlene. Now that he could identify those old pains, he was able to reappraise her nonverbal communication (as fear instead of dismissal) and see that Charlene was different from his father.

Charlene's old script was active, too. She recalled her paranoid and unpredictable mother. Early on, Charlene learned to run and hide from her mother's rage, lest her mother beat her to a pulp. For a moment, for Charlene, the rage in Ray's eyes became the threat in her mother's eyes. She began to reevaluate Ray's nonverbal cues (as humiliation instead of harm) and saw that he was nothing like her mother.

As they revealed their old scripts to each other, tenderness and compassion emerged. Vowing to take better control of his emotions, Ray reached out to embrace Charlene. Feeling more secure, she yielded and cried with relief. They left the session hand in hand.

By clearing away old scripts, Ray and Charlene's mirror neurons were less encumbered by old hurts. With better understandings of their nonverbal communication, they both felt freer to connect, which brought them greater attunement and emotional resonance.

In the next session, I asked Charlene and Ray to think of a time when they were madly in love. They recalled an impromptu picnic on the beach on a chilly fall day. To keep warm, they built a fire and huddled together, giggling and having fun. The deserted beach beckoned their imagination and their passions. They made love right then and there.

Ray's relaxed body language matched his conciliatory words. He said, "Let's go forward. I love you and I want those romantic times back."

Ray then read Charlene's nonverbal cue of strong eye contact. He interpreted that to mean warmth and affection. She confirmed Ray's thought: "I, too, want to bring back the romantic times, but I know it will take time."

In practicing these nonverbal communication exercises, Charlene and Ray have engaged more intimately with each other. They still have a ways to go, but they are on the road to reviving love and lust, to listening to both the words and the melody. And that's because words are words, but the melody—nonverbal communication—is the deeply embedded soul of the matter. That melody sings of love, and it does so neurologically.

Such fresh experiences will help you dislodge the pain entrenched in your neural circuits and replace that pain with love. By attuning with your partner authentically, you will arrive one giant step closer to empathy and intimacy.

Chapter 6

Key #4: The Healing Power of Empathy and Forgiveness

♡ Forgiving the Unforgivable

Nina recounted an interaction between her son Jon and her husband Steve. She had undergone oral surgery that day and was holding an ice pack to her swollen cheek. Although she complained repeatedly about the pain, Steve ignored her and told her about how he and Jon had a great time practicing football. He then asked her where he should put his muddy sneakers, to which she responded that he should put them anywhere—she was in agony and she really didn't care.

Nina was indeed in pain and needed comfort, but that was not evident to Steve. It was not as though Nina were vague or Steve hard of hearing. Instead, they were twenty-one years into their marriage and speaking at each other rather than to each other. You may think that this was a case of poor communication. But they communicated well when discussing events, plans, goals, friends, politics—all of which did not really entail the threatening emotions that arise in intimate dialogues. The problem arose during intimate conversations that involved empathy, at which time Steve disappeared.

Steve's failure to empathize with Nina was not an isolated incident. When Nina was pregnant with their second child, Steve had an affair. This was a time when Nina needed his assurance, support, and empathy more than ever. But his mind and body were somewhere else. Things were never the same after that. Although he tried in vain to make amends, Steve had committed a betrayal that Nina could not forgive. His offers to buy a beach house that she had always yearned for, to take her on a romantic trip to the Greek Islands, or to do anything she wanted met with bitterness. She shot back scathing sarcasm after each attempt of his to repair the damage. She simply was not having any of it. Although Nina still loved Steve, her anger and resentment eclipsed her feelings of love for him. In turning inward to heal herself, she felt nothing near empathy for Steve.

Clearly, Nina was not ready to forgive Steve for his betrayal of her and his disloyalty. And Steve was unwilling to forgive Nina for her inexorable attacks and rejection of him. Nina met his attempts to initiate sex with a dismissive "forget it," but he did not forget it, and neither did she.

Despite the discord, hurt, and betrayal between them, Nina and Steve had a long history together, and they wanted the magic, the romance back. In therapy they learned how their neural connections between empathy and forgiveness work. This understanding gave them hope that, once they restore empathy to their relationship, forgiveness will follow. Nina and Steve are working to separate the old family dynamics from their own relationship, and in doing so, they are one step closer to rewiring their brains with new patterns. And by following the exercises in this chapter, they are another step closer to repairing the relationship.

Empathy and forgiveness are of utmost importance in an intimate relationship. When you fell in love, no doubt, empathy—the ability to step into your partner's shoes while holding on to your own—was at its peak. Matching mirror neurons ensured emotional resonance between you and your partner. Your brains released chemicals to trigger feelings of love, loyalty, trust, lust, and attraction.

Alas, when love fades and a relationship becomes fraught with friction, hurt, and disappointment, the trauma withers our empathy and slows the flow of brain chemicals. Instead of walking in our partner's shoes, we dig deeply into our own shoes in an attempt to heal. This is especially so when one partner betrays the other, such as through infidelity, neglect, or abuse. Forgiveness in those cases seems nearly impossible. But forgiveness is possible. Nevertheless, there's an irony to it. If your partner betrays you, clearly he showed no empathy, yet for you to forgive him, you are required to muster empathy. And that's because forgiveness requires empathy.

A recent study documented the common neural basis

of empathy and forgiveness.[62,63] Using fMRI technology, the researchers found that neurons in certain regions of the brain fire both when we empathize and when we forgive. The results suggest, then, that the key to forgiveness is to feel empathy for your partner, maybe even when you are angry.

When you feel hurt or angry—with a conscious or unconscious wish to punish your partner for hurting you—how can you feel empathy for him, too? Revenge is more like it. If, however, you hold a grudge, constantly harass him, or withhold sex, the person you really hurt is yourself. When you punish your partner, chances are that he will feel angry with you instead of with himself. Most people feel pangs of guilt when they hurt someone they love, and so in a sense, they punish themselves. But when you punish your partner, you prevent him from punishing himself.

It's not too hard to see that forgiveness enhances relationships, but can it be good for your health, too? Studies have shown that forgiving someone instead of holding a grudge enhances emotional and physical health and reduces physiological responses to the hurt inflicted.[64] If forgiveness is a good thing all around, how then do you forgive someone who's hurt you terribly? There are three steps to arrive at being able to forgive:

1. Empathy
2. Repair
3. Humility

EMPATHY

The power of interacting mirror neurons to trigger empathy between your partner and you will become evident. You will eventually be able to attune to each other's internal states and feelings, including shame, sadness, anxiety, fear, trauma, pain, loneliness, anger, bitterness, and despair. During this process of empathizing, it is most important that the offender—either you or your partner—experience the hurt of the offended to feel true remorse and guilt. The following exercises draw on the example of pain that your partner has inflicted on you, but as I've mentioned before, the shoe may have been on the other foot, or the hurt may be for different reasons. First, get in touch with your inner feelings, whether disappointment, pain related to a devastating blow to your self-esteem, sadness, despair, anger, fear, or something else. Let the feelings wash over you and take the time to feel empathy for yourself. Then:

- Explain to your partner how you felt when he hurt you. Don't try to be cool by holding back the full range of emotions. Let it all out, calmly.

- Ask your partner to put himself in your shoes and pretend this happened to him. What would he be feeling then? Can he resonate with your feelings?

- Listen to your partner's response. If he tries to defend or explain himself, stop him and tell him that this is about his empathy for you. His turn will come later, when you will empathize with his feelings.

- At this point, your partner will, no doubt, offer an

apology. By reading his nonverbal cues and verbal communication, you will be better able to know whether his apology is sincere.

- Ask him what he feels about hurting you. Once you recognize that he has shown remorse and is feeling some guilt, you are on the way to repair.

REPAIR

Making amends is the best way for your partner to help you repair your pain and to appease his feelings of guilt. Before your partner can begin to repair the damage, you must get in touch with your needs and express them to your partner. For example, you may want more attention, romance, closeness, thoughtfulness, empathy, or attunement to your emotions, desires, goals, or intentions.

Once you are in touch with your needs, tell your partner exactly what they are. At this point in the process, your partner most likely wants to make amends so that he can repair the damage. Help him by explaining that he not only should talk about how he feels but also should show you with actions what he will do to make amends.

HUMILITY

You are almost at the finish line of forgiveness, but first you must empathize with your partner. Even if he didn't empathize with you when you needed it, now he should

show empathy and remorse and try to repair the damage.
Once you can understand, feel, and experience where your
partner is coming from, it is easier to imagine yourself in a
vulnerable place—one that is similar to but different from
that of your partner, one that is your own vulnerable place.

Humility is the last step before forgiveness. Try to humble yourself by thinking of times when you hurt someone,
whether or not it was intentional. Get in touch with your
own shortcomings and anger, and with how those may
have affected others. Although you may not think that
your offenses rise to the level of your partner's, they nevertheless hurt someone. Just as your partner is fallible, so
are you—we all are.

At this point, you are probably almost ready to forgive
him, to let go of the pain, the hurt, the revenge fantasies,
and the anger. If pride is still in the way, go back in time
and recall the love, the romance, the good times, your own
frailties, your hurtful words and actions. The more you
reach a deeper level of humility, the easier it will be to
forgive your partner.

FORGIVENESS

Now that you have arrived at a healing place of empathy
and forgiveness for your partner, it is his turn. No doubt,
the pain he caused you met with your ire. Chances are that
he feels angry with you about the pain you inflicted on him,
too. Now he must let go of his pain and anger, empathize

with you, and forgive you. To do this, repeat the previous exercises but reverse them. Put yourself in your partner's shoes and empathize with his feelings—his perception of himself as the aggrieved and you as the offender. He can execute the three steps of empathy, repair, and humility so that you can forgive him.

Let's return to Nina and Steve's story to see how this process of empathy and forgiveness plays out in a real-life couple. Nina and Steve had both read the exercises and were trying to immerse themselves in the process. Nina tried in vain to hide her sorrow, pain, and anger: "When I found out, I fell apart. I kept shaking and crying, and I was unable to eat or sleep. I just couldn't pull myself together."

Steve lowered his eyes and bowed his head: "I am so sorry," he muttered.

It wasn't enough for Nina: "I was seven months pregnant with your baby—how could you do it? I was feeling fat and undesirable. I should have been feeling on top of the world. We wanted this baby so much; instead, I felt so low, so rejected. Why'd you do it?"

Steve winced: "I don't know why I did it. I was stupid."

Nina crossed her arms and spoke up: "How would you feel if the shoe was on the other foot? If I cheated on you when you were feeling vulnerable?"

"I would feel terrible," Steve responded quickly. "Like my manhood was assailed. If Nina cheated with another man, I guess I'd feel like I was not good enough. But what about how I feel when she rejects me sexually?"

Nina flashed, "See how he turns everything around to himself?"

After I reminded him that it was his turn to empathize with Nina, Steve offered: "I love you more than anything or anyone in the world, and I can't believe I hurt the most precious thing in my life. Please forgive me. I'm so sorry. I want to make it up to you. Give me a chance."

But Nina was not ready to do that. Wringing her hands in anguish, Nina stared at Steve and asked, "How can I trust you again? Maybe you're still seeing her or you want to see her. What does she have going for her that I don't have?"

"Nothing. She means nothing to me. We've been through this over and over. Please let it go and give us a chance. It's been ten years."

Part of the reason Nina was having such a difficult time in forgiving Steve was that her anger was not letting her go forward. The more Nina obsessed about Steve's affair, the angrier she became. For her to move on, we had to bring positive thoughts into her mind. I encouraged her to get in touch with what she needed and desired from Steve.

She directed herself at Steve: "For one thing, I need empathy, kindness, consideration, and mostly that you get out of your head and into mine. Like when you ignored the pain in my mouth and talked about what you needed. You didn't understand what I needed from you. A warm shoulder, that's what I needed."

Reaching out to Nina, Steve countered, "I want to give you all of that, but I can't. When you rejected me sexually, I was traumatized. It's not that I can't feel empathy for you again, but I was so devastated and angry with you that I couldn't think about your feelings. And now I take full responsibility for the dumb thing I did, but you need to see how you keep on hurting me. You're still punishing me for a mistake I made ten years ago." His voice grew hoarse.

To help Nina move on to the positive experience of forgiveness, I asked whether she could imagine herself hurting someone else, even inadvertently.

Lowering her head, Nina responded, "Yes, I have, and I feel so guilty and ashamed of it. When I was a kid, the other kids dared me to punch a younger, intellectually disabled kid in the nose. I guess I was showing off and wanted their approval so I rose to the dare. It was a terrible mistake. I have a hard time forgiving myself for it." This early childhood memory of shame and guilt was embedded in the brain and still hurt when it emerged,

Nina agreed to try to forgive herself and to try to forgive Steve. This was indeed a new way of thinking for her, and it would create new neural pathways and allow her to change her reactions to new situations. Steve felt that his mirror neurons were reflecting Nina's pain, and he didn't waste a minute: "I understand how you felt, and I want to try to forgive you for hurting me back. I think the day my father died, all hell broke loose."

Steve and Nina reached forgiveness by being able to empathize with each other. Although they each came from different backgrounds, with their fair shares of family ghosts, they were united in their wish to repair their relationship.

Nina's self-esteem was on shaky ground, and when Steve cheated, it nearly toppled her self-esteem entirely. When Steve understood why Nina held on to the pain, he found empathy for her and then he also found it in himself to forgive her.

The steps to forgiveness don't always move in an orderly fashion. For Nina and Steve, there were some detours on the road to forgiveness. Fortunately, with new thoughtful and loving experiences, Nina and Steve are able to create new patterns of relating and rewire old neural pathways. Because mirror neurons reflect negative and positive feelings to partners in an intimate relationship, if you dislike your partner and feel angry, mirror neurons will reflect that dislike and anger. The upside of mirror neurons is that when your partner feels remorseful and loving, his mirror neurons will reflect those feelings to you. By reflecting to each other empathy, humility, repair, and forgiveness, Nina and Steve can enjoy better times together in the present and look forward to a brighter future.

Each of us is unique, and so every story has its own beginning, middle, and end. Unfortunately, not every story has a happy ending like that of Nina and Steve. Not everyone is willing to reach deep inside their minds and souls to feel guilt, to repent, and to make amends. But my hope is that you find the inner strength to create change in yourself. As you do, mirror neurons will reflect your strengths to your partner and encourage change, but it may not be the change you would like. If your partner does choose to create change, then look deeply into your heart and mind to find the empathy to forgive him. If you can hold hands on the road to recovery, your matching mirror neurons and enhanced brain chemicals will pave the way, bringing you one step closer to rewiring your brain and rekindling intimate feelings.

There is nothing quite like the power of empathy, humility, and forgiveness to move you and your partner forward even in the most difficult situations. Such was the case for Julie and Alex, whose story proves that forgiveness can be difficult.

♡ The Saint and the Sinner

Before she could sit down, Julie's angry words tumbled out: "He's drinking again. And gambling. You should've seen him yesterday. He was drunk as a skunk. He took off all his clothes in the yard in front of the neighbors and ran out in the street. He's a disgusting pig just like his alcoholic mother."

Alex responded softly, "I don't know what she's talking about. I wasn't even drinking. She makes up stories."

If Julie was angry when she walked in, she was now on the verge of exploding. "I can't stand you! Our kids want me to divorce you, and I'm going to do that."

Alex tried to extinguish his wife's fury: "I'll stop drinking and gambling. I promise I will."

"Your promises are empty, just like you. You're an empty shell," responded Julie. She would not be placated so easily.

Alex and Julie began to provoke each other, bringing up events from the past, especially the time that Alex had cheated on her. I encouraged Julie to tell Alex how she felt.

"He won't get it. All he thinks about is himself."

Alex tried to appease her: "I think about you all the time. Babe, you're the best."

"I don't believe him for even one moment," said Julie.

I asked Alex what he thought Julie was feeling. He bellowed, "I think she's a mean, angry woman who enjoys beating me down. I'm hurting, too. And I told her I won't drink anymore."

Julie shook her head in disbelief and said, "He's been saying that for thirty-two years of our marriage. He began drinking at age ten with his mother. She treated him like her boyfriend, not like her son."

"I don't have to listen to this anymore!" Alex yelled. "I'm out of here."

I encouraged Alex to cool down for a minute. Then he reached out to Julie and said more calmly, "I'm sorry, Julie. Like I said, I won't do it again."

Julie remained silent. I asked whether she thought Alex was sorry. She responded, "No, not at all. He says 'I'm sorry' so fast and I say 'OK' and then he does it again. I don't trust him. But there's another part. When he sobers up, Alex is the sweetest, most loving, attentive husband and father."

"I love you so much," Alex said, smiling.

"I love you, too, but you're driving me crazy. Your behavior has to change."

Looking despondent, Alex spoke in a mellow voice: "I really do want to change. I know that when I feel low, I drink, and that's not a good thing. But when Julie insults me like she does, I feel lower than ever, so I drink again."

I helped Alex and Julie to see that when Alex was drinking and gambling, she disconnected from her love for him and became enraged. And when he was on good behavior, she disconnected from the rage she felt earlier and went on to love him dearly. That troubled interaction kept repeating itself. Even when they would make up, it was temporary. To make lasting change, they had to work on changing how they interact with each other. In all the anger, resentment, hurt, and pain that they were inflicting on each other, they lost sight of any understanding of the other person, where that person was coming from and what he or she was feeling. They had no empathy. But without empathy, they couldn't forgive or heal each other, and they couldn't bring real, consistent love back into a relationship.

In later sessions, we worked on empathy, repair, humility, and forgiveness. First, we worked on empathy. A look back at their childhoods helped Julie and Alex gain a better understanding of and compassion toward each other, which brought them one step closer to empathy and rewiring their neural pathways.

Julie felt sorry for Alex, whose mother exploited him and robbed him of his adolescence. She saw that he was unconsciously acting out his reckless adolescence. Recognizing the roots of his behavior helped Julie to some extent, but she was still in terrible pain. It was nearly impossible for her to garner empathy for Alex, who had never showed empathy for her. Nevertheless, she wanted to repair the relationship.

Julie let her feelings wash over her—humiliation, anger, hurt, despair, and the blow to her self-esteem. After allowing herself to feel empathy for herself, she expressed her feelings to Alex. Then Alex put himself in Julie's shoes and imagined what he would feel. Although he tried to defend himself once or twice, he quickly got back on track. Resonating with her feelings, he was able to get in touch with his regret and remorse. When he apologized again, Julie read his verbal and nonverbal cues and felt that he was sincere.

We reversed this exercise, so that Alex could see the damage Julie's alcoholic father had created for her and how her mother had caved in and suffered in silence. Determined not to follow in her mother's footsteps, Julie vehemently tried to control Alex's behavior. Of course, only Alex could control his behavior. When Alex recognized the origin of Julie's actions, he was able to empathize with her.

When I asked Alex to get in touch with the feelings

that arise when Julie heaps insults on him, he described depression, low self-worth, and humiliation. In the past, those feelings drove him to drink. When Julie put herself in Alex's shoes, she began to cry. She told Alex that she felt guilty about her role in the relationship and that she would try to change. He reacted with a tender smile of gratitude.

The next step was repair. As already described, the best way to make amends is to go into action and try to repair your partner's hurt feelings. In this case, Alex, who had first rejected the idea of getting help for his drinking and gambling problem, volunteered to enroll in an inpatient rehabilitation center. He later completed the program and remained sober. His change could not have occurred without change in Julia. Rather than reminding him constantly about his terrible treatment of her, Julie worked on empathy and began to behave in a caring, supportive way.

To address humility, I asked Julie to think of a time she hurt someone else, and she did not go any further than her demeaning behavior with Alex. The shame she felt was indeed humbling. Of course, Alex also felt guilty and ashamed of his hurtful behavior with his friends, family, and Julia. Things were looking up.

Julie and Alex seemed to sail off happily into the sunset together. The sea, however, could be rough and the going bumpy, but with good stewardship, they could reach their destination. Alex slipped up sometimes, but he was honest about it and took control quickly. Julia had transformed her anger to patience, tolerance, and empathy. She no longer disconnected the good from the bad but was aware that, when things were going well, they were not necessarily perfect or permanent. And when things went awry, they still had their underlying love and devotion.

Their new interaction was, in part, due to neural plasticity: as they changed how they related to each other, their brains were able to find new patterns, to rewire themselves. The dopamine receptors in Alex's brain that craved alcohol and risky behavior—part of the pleasure-reward system—became calmer. His relationship with Julie began to give him a new kind of pleasure. These days, he is no longer acting out his adolescent abandon but is behaving responsibly. The hope of repairing her relationship is helping Julie to heal from her old pain.

With mirror neurons reflecting their inner states, as Julie brings out the best in Alex, he brings out the best in her. And once again their mirror neurons trigger the release of good-mood and love-enhancing brain chemicals, which bring them into greater intimacy with each other.

Although the examples in this chapter are dramatic ones of how couples can hurt each other, partners can generate pain more subtly, too. For example, if your children or career are demanding, you may unwittingly neglect your partner's needs, making him feel slighted and hurt. He may then lash out at you, and before you know it, your interactions are marred. If this or any other problematic interaction is impairing intimacy in your relationship, then you can take the steps to forgiveness: savor your strength while facing your faults, learn from the past, communicate your needs, and learn empathy and forgiveness. These four keys will help unlock your brain from its unproductive patterns of relating.

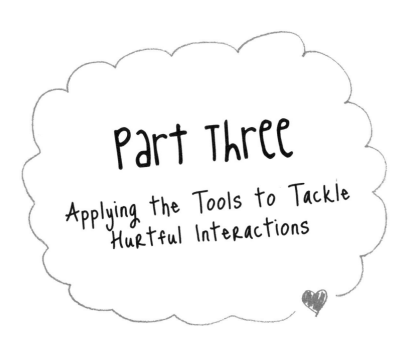

part Three

Applying the Tools to Tackle Hurtful Interactions

you have acquired the skills needed to tackle repetitive hurtful interactions, and now you are ready to apply those tools to change three relationship traps. When you can change these deeply ingrained, hurtful interactions, you will change your neural pathways as well. Rather than change at a fleeting cognitive and surface level, the change you will learn here occurs at a deep emotional and neural level.

When you find yourself in a relationship trap, mirror neurons—which reflect partners' inner worlds of feelings to each other—work in a special way. They not only reflect similar feelings, thoughts, and intentions but also reflect opposite ones. Remember that your partner is his own person, and so his inner world—of thoughts, feelings, and intentions—is not necessarily the same as yours. Whether or not you are similar, mirror neurons reflect your partner's inner world to you as though you were reading his mind. The reverse is true also: mirror neurons reflect your inner world to your partner as though he were reading your mind.

You can bridge your differences and incorporate those differences into your repertoire for growth. In this type of healthy interaction, mirror neurons reflect differences that are complementary to partners. Mirror neurons, however, can connect to disparate traits in partners so that unequal powers become polarized. Indeed, polarizing interactions, no matter how subtle, are a setup for a dynamic of domination and submission, which can erode your self-esteem and destroy a relationship. You will learn how to recognize this interaction of unequal powers and how to change it to one of equality.

Another prevalent relationship dynamic is negative fortune-telling, which happens when we unconsciously disavow the characteristics that we dislike in ourselves and project them onto our partners. We unwittingly behave in a way that provokes our partners to act out those characteristics; instead of satisfaction, strife sets in. The tools you master in this part will help you untangle yourself from this dreaded spiral. By accepting all parts of yourself—the good, the bad, and the ugly—you will see how you can change the interactions in your relationship to become more fulfilling.

This part will show you how, even though you are able to bring love back to your relationship, it's still a struggle to kindle the passion. You will learn about some of the motivations for this disconnect of love and lust. Then I present some exercises to help your mirror neurons and brain chemicals recruit the sexiness and tenderness in you.

unequal powers, unequal partners

THE CHOREOGRAPHY OF CONTROL

In part 2, you learned how to visit the past so that it does not distort the present, to build a stronger sense of self, to communicate verbally and nonverbally for your needs to be met, and to find healing through empathy and forgiveness. In the process, your mirror neurons have reflected more loving feelings between you and your partner. As a result, you are now armed with a stockpile of tools and skills but also with better-oiled mirror neurons and brain chemistry.

By now you've gained an understanding of the neurology and psychology of love and how mirror neurons operate, so you know that when you repair your relationship, you can rewire those neural pathways. If you find yourself in a relationship trap, you can apply those skills to change things. The first trap we'll talk about is unequal powers, which erode women's self-esteem and destroy relationships.

In an unequal power relationship, one partner dominates and the other submits; that is, one partner forgoes his
or her needs, wishes, and desires and caves in to the other.
In this dynamic, one partner controls the other partner's
opinions, feelings, friends, and activities; the other partner
simply capitulates.

On the surface, the controlling partner seems to be the
strong one and the submissive partner the weak one. Dig a
little deeper, though, and you will find that both partners
are equally weak. Although their behavior is opposite to
each other, they are similar in their inner fragility. And
the fragility of partners entwined in a dynamic of control
and submission—whether derived from unresolved family issues or societal messages—inevitably centers on the
unconscious fear of abandonment.

Here's how it plays out: Both partners unconsciously
fear that they will be left alone. The domineering partner,
in this case, the man, imagines that if he controls his partner he knows exactly how, what, and where she is. That
way, she can't leave him, and he feels safe. In turn, the
submissive partner imagines that if she caves in her partner won't leave her.

Let's peek in on the reality of this lopsided relationship. The controlling partner, typically the man, swallows up the submissive partner, typically the woman,
who caves into him. Mirror neuron systems move on to
a one-way street as the controlling partner dominates the
messages exchanged between the two brains. The woman

no longer feels that she exists as a separate person, and the man feels left alone. As such, neither partner has someone to get real feedback from ideas; to share inner feelings and thoughts that differ; to discuss diverse opinions, events, or philosophies. With one person dominating the interaction, there is no potential for emotional attunement and empathic resonance.

It can happen the other way around, too. A woman may be the domineering partner who swallows up the man, while the man is the submissive partner who collapses into her. In either case, one partner ceases to exist and leaves the other partner alone, and this puts a halt to intimate relating. To bring love back to a relationship, intimate partners must be separate people with equal power. A healthy relationship requires mutuality so that mirror neurons can properly reflect messages and feelings back and forth.

For the most part, men dominate and women submit. Despite the influence of feminism, of women's empowerment in the workplace, of female politicians running for president, unequal power relations live on. For women to empower themselves, to gain respect and recognition from their partners, they must embrace certain fundamental rights—and that starts with their entitlement to an equal power relationship with mutuality and reciprocity.

Part of the problem in unequal power relationships stems from traditional family dynamics, which continue to influence our self-image in adulthood. Young girls require not only strong, independent mothers with whom to identify but also strong, independent fathers. When fathers are emotionally or physically unavailable, girls identify with the more available parent, in this case, mothers. Too often, they identify with a selfless mother who is not a subject of her own but an object to meet her family's needs.

The issue of sexual desire is also on the table. A domineering man takes on the active role of sexually desiring a woman, whereas a submissive woman takes on the passive role of being desired by a man. For young women to develop a sense of themselves as independent and strong, their parents must validate their growing into womanhood.

Things, however, are not so black and white. Women who embrace their own needs and desires must also nurture themselves and devote themselves to their loved ones. But women also need power, autonomy, achievement, and independence, which traditionally are found in the domain of men. Power is not gendered; both men and women need it.[65]

With one foot stuck in the past, women may feel that their disparate needs create conflict. The need for power, independence, and achievement remains at odds with their wish for protection, financial security, and comfort in the company of a man. How can a woman have it all? For a Pyrrhic victory, she can forgo her own power and independence, submit to an idealized powerful man, and derive her power vicariously through him. But, in this way, she has set the table for male domination and abuse of power. The couple is no longer two separate, independent

partners—and the relationship does not represent intimacy. Indeed, intimate relationships require that two
separate, independent partners are interdependent.

Achieving mutual empathic resonance and emotional
attunement—which can flourish only in equal power
relationships—is key to relationship repair. To arrive at an
equal power relationship, stereotypical female and stereotypical male roles live side by side.

Rather than male domination and female submission,
hurting or being hurt, doing to or having done to, desiring or being desired, with resonating mirror neurons, each
partner can embrace both roles—that's what an equal
power relationship is about.

Financial issues can also affect how couples negotiate
power. In today's economy, where families often need two
salaries to make ends meet, equal power relationships are
more important than ever. To stay afloat financially, mil-
lions of married women with children find themselves
in the workplace. It certainly sounds like equality—this
two-person working couple. But all may not be rosy, and
before you know it, the balance tips.

♡ Sarah's Sad Story

Sarah and Len's mirror neurons connect them in a dynamic
of control and submission, but with a modern-day twist.
Both have demanding careers, and both work hard. On
the surface, their mirror neurons reflect similarities, but at

a deeper level, trouble is brewing. They entered therapy to resolve some of their issues.

"I'm bored with my work, and I want more of a challenge," Sarah ventured tentatively.

Len barked, "What're you talking about? We've been there before. No way are you going back to working all hours and leaving me to take care of the kids. I remember how I became your slave. It's out of the question."

Raised in a traditional male-breadwinner home, Len refused to accept that his family needed two salaries to make ends meet. The fact that Sarah made more money than Len was an additional threat to him. And now that she was proposing making even more money, Len felt even more powerless.

But then there were Sarah's feelings. Not only was her salary a necessity; she loved her work. She felt valued, recognized, and appreciated there. And so the dilemma arose: to work or not to work.

Of course, working moms today have options. Many get a nanny for the children, disregard their husbands' complaints, and pursue their own ambitions for autonomy and equal power. Sarah—a young, brilliant attorney—could not do that. Instead, she turned herself inside out to please her husband. For example, Sarah, who was influenced by her family upbringing and societal messages, said, "What's a loving wife to do when her husband is so upset? I know I have to please him. After all, I love him. But I do everything I can think of, and nothing's working! I'm exhausted.

I come home from work and cook, clean, shop. You know what he does? He reads or watches TV. The only thing he helps me with is the kids. He likes playing sports with them. If I ask him to shop, cook, or clean, he tells me that he's the slave and I'm the master. That hurts. In my family, my father was in charge, not my mother."

Influenced by her family dynamics, Sarah felt ashamed that she was not pleasing her husband. As a result, unconsciously, she overdid her efforts to please Len. She insisted on fulfilling Len's wishes that she cook, clean, shop, and attend to the children's needs. Feeling guilty for causing Len distress on the one hand and wishing to succeed in her career on the other hand, Sarah was torn. Even though she continued to shine at work, at home she had become a slave. In turn, Len had become the master. In this uncanny way, they together played out the scripts of control and submission.

Sarah and Len were able to rectify their problems, change their dynamic of unequal power, and rewire their brains. They learned that their mirror neurons were locked into some unproductive and hurtful patterns of behavior. They worked on the four keys to unlock the brain described in part 2, with the aim of writing new, healthy behavioral patterns to modify their neural pathways.

The process began with Sarah, who addressed the first key by visiting the past. An old scenario featuring her disapproving mother came to her mind. Her mother had disapproved of a neighbor, Betty, whom she accused of putting work ahead of her children. "Can you imagine what'll become of these kids? I'll bet they'll drop out of school, do drugs, and land in jail—or they'll kill themselves." In her mind, Sarah had become Betty.

As Sarah learned, however, life often gets in the way, and things have a way of changing over time. Len's salary as a high school teacher did not suffice, which made the need for two salaries a necessity. Sarah's earning power as an attorney and her need for greater independence propelled her back to work.

Sarah thought that she was turning into Betty, and with her mother's disapproving voice in her head, her old script was impinging on her relationship with Len. The conclusion she came to was that she was not Betty and that she was not obligated to follow her mother's dictates. This insight helped her to rewire her brain and to revise the relationship with Len.

Sarah was overworked, stressed, and unhappy, and it became apparent that she was sabotaging herself. Determined to eliminate her mother's messages from her repertoire, Sarah felt entitled to an equal division of labor at home. Rather than backing down to Len's demands, she has begun to delegate household chores to him. When he balks, Sarah tells Len that she needs him and that she has faith that he can help her. He eventually agrees, and then she lets him know what a great man he is.

In working on the second key to relationship repair—savoring her strengths and facing her faults—Sarah is

replacing her role model of her selfless mother with other
role models, <u>women who excel at home and at work and</u>
<u>who value themselves</u>. Rather than simply doing things
for her family, she is doing fun things for herself. She has
resumed some old hobbies and is socializing more with
friends. As she proceeds, she is valuing her flexibility, the
fact that she can create changes, that she can be kind to
herself and to others, and that she can function on an
equal footing with people in her profession and with Len
in her personal life.

Len joined Sarah for the third key—practicing verbal
and nonverbal communication. Sarah found that when
she was at work, her words and nonverbal cues depicted
a self-assured, direct, independent woman; at home,
however, her communication depicted her as an insecure,
hesitant, and selfless woman. This awareness helped her
change how she communicated with Len. <u>As she conveys</u>
<u>her needs and desires to him in a more self-confident and</u>
<u>forthright way, Len is beginning to respond in a more</u>
<u>accepting and cooperative way.</u>

When Sarah stopped trying so hard to please her husband by sacrificing herself, Len became supportive and
has tried to please her. This new turn of events is helping
Len rewrite the definition of a powerful man whose wife
pleases him to one of a powerful man who can actually
please an accomplished woman like Sarah.

Finally, Sarah and Len worked on repairing the relationship further with the fourth key: eliciting empathy

and forgiveness. They both felt remorse over the barbs they hurled at one another, the attacks, the dismissals, the silent treatment, and the fiery exchanges—all of which blocked their empathy for each other. Now that they have practiced how to walk in each other's shoes, to make amends for their roles in the troubled relationship, and to dig down into their inner selves and find humility, they have begun to forgive each other and move forward. With mirror neurons reflecting their inner worlds to each other, Len and Sarah have gone from a dynamic of control and submission—of unequal powers—to one of equality.

Sarah and Len's story shows one way that a power struggle can degrade love and intimacy; there are many others. Another way that a power struggle degrades intimacy is the dependency trap.

THE DEPENDENCY TRAP

It's one of the most common problems in a relationship: mirror neurons connect partners in a dynamic of male independence, competence, and autonomy, and female dependence, inadequacy, and extreme submission. Indeed, in most cases, women feel dependent on the men in their lives. In some instances, however, men fear depending on women.

If any of this is true in your relationship, then you know how emotional or financial dependency can make you fear that you're losing yourself in your partner and can contribute to feelings of inadequacy. At the surface level, such dependency can be comforting, yet at a deeper level, it can be demoralizing. Conversely, if your partner depends on you, you may feel burdened and resentful; you may feel that you're stroking your partner's ego by pretending to depend on him. This may make you feel compromised and angry.

If your relationship is caught in the dependency trap, what old scripts are at play? Maybe one of your parents was overindulgent, overprotective, or coddling. Maybe a parent blamed the teacher when you failed a test or automatically took your side when you had a fight with a friend. Sound familiar? If so, what script did you write as a result?

You may have resisted your parents' overprotection and learned to take care of yourself at an early age. As an adult, your script was about functioning independently and autonomously, and experiencing yourself as competent and masterful.

If, however, you enjoyed the overprotection and basked in your parents' attentions and persistent ministrations, you probably wrote a vastly different script. In this old script, chances are that you never developed a sense of self-mastery. Perhaps one parent or the other was the master of your fate, making all your decisions for you—the college you attended, the studies you pursued, the friends you hung out with. As a result, you didn't have to make any decisions of your own. Your parents took you under their wing, overshadowed you, kept you effectively incon-sequential. Today, though, you may feel woefully inad-equate or unable to take care of yourself, let alone depend on yourself.

So, what are you to do? Let's take a look at the story of Courtney and Al.

♡ Delicate and Daring

Courtney's dark eyes clouded up with distress: "I'm so miserable in this relationship. It's not like I didn't try to fix it. We tried marriage counseling, and even though Al chose the therapist, he walked out in the second session."

"So he calls the shots?" I asked. "Is that why you're so distressed?"

Courtney responded, "Not exactly. I like that Al takes charge. It makes me feel protected, safe. I look up to his power: he's a sharp businessman, he makes all the social arrangements, and he pays all the bills."

I asked, "Why, then, are you so unhappy?"

"For one thing, he's critical of my cellulite. He tells me to exercise more and watches everything I eat. And he doesn't trust me with money. He says I spend too much of it. I guess it's true, so he's got a right to insist that he control the money. I have to ask him for money and keep the receipts so he can check them."

I offered, "So he treats you like a child?"

"I guess so, but I'm terrible with money," she giggled.

"And as for the cellulite, my legs don't look like they did when we met. He looks different, too, but he's a guy, so it doesn't matter."

I asked Courtney whether she thought she held a double standard about looks and gender roles in relationships. She remarked, "I never thought of it that way. All I know is that I'm not happy with Al, and I'm happy with Jim. He's my voice teacher. He's helping me get my voice back in shape. Before I met Al, I studied opera. I performed in local venues, and my teachers told me I was good enough to perform all over the world. But I gave it all up to marry Al and have kids. Al thinks now it's a waste of time. But there's a big problem here. I fell in love with Jon."

Courtney began to describe Jim: "He's deep and sensitive, so we have long conversations, not only about music but about lots of things. He values my opinions, my talent, and my tenacity." For a moment, she shone with self-assurance. The moment, however, was short lived. I tried to help Courtney work out whether she was really in love with Jim or could still repair her relationship with Al.

In therapy, Courtney examined the old script that she had written with her parents as a young child. She remembered her overprotective mother and controlling father. Her mother was an anxious, fearful woman who worried that Courtney's diminutive body meant she wasn't strong. She constantly warned her not to tax herself by studying too much at school or by overworking herself in sports. Her mother's treatment of Courtney like a delicate hothouse plant did little to help her feel anything but fragile. "You're so beautiful you'll find a rich man to take care of you, just like I did," her mother assured her. And indeed, just like her mother, Courtney had married a wealthy man twenty years her senior who was in charge of everything.

Before long, Courtney began to take stock of her strengths, her talents, her intelligence. She realized that she could rewrite the old script of herself as fragile, incompetent, and helpless. She began to value not only her outer beauty but also her inner beauty—her kind, caring, and loving traits. By savoring her strengths, she can face her faults, including her fear of independence. A part-time job as an assistant voice teacher is one way she is testing the waters of independence and self-reliance. Making a decision on her own, without input from Al or Jim, is another way that she can feel more autonomous and powerful.

Courtney eventually made the big decision to put her relationship with Jim on hold so that she could focus on her marriage. Although Al would not join her in couples therapy, she worked on how to communicate verbally and nonverbally in ways that reflected her feelings of greater confidence and competence. Courtney was able to empathize with Al and his need to control her, and she was even willing to forgive him.

As I've said previously, change in one partner alters the conditions so that the other partner will change in some way as well. Those ways may or may not be instrumental in relationship repair and rewiring. There is no guarantee of success, because deep change takes deep commitment and diligence. Whereas Courtney was determined to create change, Al refused to participate and dug in his heels deeper than ever. His behavior became even more toxic to the relationship. Mirror neurons that reflected Courtney's changes to Al were not reciprocated by Al's mirror neurons; instead of interacting on a two-way street, Al was on a different street altogether.

Courtney tried to communicate her needs to Al, but he wasn't having it. The stronger and more independent she felt, the more threatened Al felt. The more she tried to stand her ground, the more Al tried to control and to demoralize her. One not-so-fine day, when Al could not get his way, he pushed Courtney down a flight of stairs. Although he picked her up and took her to the emergency room, he showed no remorse. Forgiving Al—who insisted that she made him do it—was no longer in Courtney's repertoire. She had already sought the advice of a lawyer, and the following day she filed for divorce. Courtney has moved from a delicate flower to a daring woman who is taking her own life in her hands.

What exactly did Courtney do about her relationship with Jim? She came to the conclusion that she was not ready to become deeply involved with any man until she felt more independent financially and emotionally. Jim was certainly a catalyst for change in how Courtney felt about herself and about Al, but she needed time alone first. Her brain had to rewire itself so she could move on from the dependency trap that she had fallen into with Al.

Courtney and Al are an example of how unequal powers erode self-esteem and impair relationships. Take stock of the unique way power struggle figures into your relationship. Then trace the societal influences and your old scripts with a controlling or submissive parent. Can you see how old family and societal scripts are putting a damper on your love life? Eliminate them and change your focus to bringing equality and intimacy back to your relationship. The following sections provide some ways for you to do so.

Become Aware of Unequal Powers in Your Relationship

For some of us, unequal powers are apparent, but for others, although we feel uncomfortable, we are not in touch with the discrepancy in power as the source of our discomfort. Influenced by social and family scripts, some of us may deny that this unequal power dynamic exists.

Get in Touch with Your Role in Your Relationship

You may feel that you are the helpless victim in an unequal relationship, but maybe you are unaware of how you allowed it to happen. For example, maybe you were taught to please men at all cost, to cave in to their demands, or to give yourself selflessly to their needs and desires. Or maybe you simply enjoy the financial benefits of dependence and reliance on a man. Once you can get in touch with your role, you are poised to begin the process of inner change and relationship change.

Imagine a More Equal Power Relationship

How does it feel when your partner tries to please you or respects your needs, desires, intentions, thoughts, and feelings? If you find it strange, there is a reason for this feeling—an old dynamic of inequality has become entrenched in your neural pathways. Remember, your brain is plastic—it can be shaped and reshaped, wired and rewired—so that by following the keys presented in the preceding chapters, you can realign the neural pathways in your brain.

Reclaim Your Power

An unequal power dynamic has, no doubt, eroded your self-esteem. It is thus essential that you begin to reclaim your power and embrace your strengths, your virtues, your talents, and your ability to love and nurture (see chapter 4). Enlist the friendship of other women who are struggling with similar issues and finding ways to empower themselves. Begin the process of self-care by joining a gym, maintaining a nutritious diet, taking classes, or going back to work. As you begin to feel more empowered, your self-esteem will improve and you will begin to feel comfortable about asking your partner to meet your needs.

Practice Verbal and Nonverbal Communication Skills

Engage your partner in a dialogue in which you can communicate verbally and nonverbally without blaming or attacking him. Describe your feelings to him, and ask him to try to put himself in your shoes. When you think he understands your needs, ask him to explain his needs without blaming or attacking you. You can follow the exercises in chapter 5.

Practice Empathy and Forgiveness

Explain clearly what has been hurtful and what you need in your relationship. Check to see whether your partner shows remorse and feels guilty about the pain he inflicted on you. If he does feel guilty, it's time to empathize with him and begin the healing process of forgiveness. If you have hurt him, now is the time to acknowledge it, feel the pain of guilt, and ask for his forgiveness.

As hopeful as this may sound, there are extreme cases of unequal powers that are exceedingly challenging. One of the most egregious types of control and submission is known as a sadomasochistic dynamic. Meet Stacy and Rob, whose unequal power relationship catapulted them smack into a difficult case.

The Stripper and Her Savior

The one-time topless dancer and coke addict, tough talking Stacy was now threatening suicide. I pleaded with her to go straight to the emergency room, at which she began to sob and give me assurances that she would not do anything to harm herself. Although Stacy had never attempted suicide, she had always suffered from lackluster moods, and she was currently struggling with a serotonin deficit and depression. A live-wire act of risky behavior and cocaine use had previously kept her tottering on a perilous dopamine high.

Dopamine is a pleasure-giving neurotransmitter. Using drugs like cocaine or engaging in risky or exciting behaviors triggers the brain to release more dopamine. A fatigued, depressed, and downtrodden person instantly gets a surge of energy, euphoria, and confidence.[66] Without having to work for it, a person can transform a boring, dreary life into a thrilling one. A powerless loser suddenly feels like a powerful winner. What could possibly compete with a dopamine high?

Unfortunately, the high is short lived, which leaves the dopamine receptors that are primed to receive the dopamine depleted and hungry. The brain develops a tolerance to the risky behavior, so it takes more and more of that behavior to achieve thrilling highs.

In a short time, occasional sniffs of cocaine failed to give Stacy the highs she loved, so she upped the quantity and soared right into addiction. It took a heart-attack scare for her to come to her senses. When Stacy worked at a strip club, the power and thrill she felt from taunting men with her body soon waned, and she felt lower than ever. The dark alley of prostitution was not far off, when she met Rob, an exciting, brooding man of difficult moods and easy money who made her heart skip a beat.

Part of the excitement for Stacy lay in Rob's risky profession. A professional gambler, he took his wins and losses seriously and his women casually. With Rob's big bucks, expensive gifts, and lavish lifestyle, Stacy was on top of the world. She retired from her own escapades and derived her thrills vicariously through Rob. Alas, it didn't last long. Rob's heavy gambling losses led to the pawn shop, trouble buying groceries, and foreclosure on their eight-thousand-square-foot home.

The financial losses, being out of work, and withdrawal from drugs brought with them a resounding dopamine crash that plummeted Stacy down to earth. Refusing medication, Stacy looked to Rob to save her. But Rob couldn't even save himself, let alone Stacy.

In a therapy session, Stacy's teary eyes fell to the floor. Her cell phone rang, but she didn't answer it. Then she said, "I'm sorry I forgot to turn it off. It's so like me these days. I don't have my wits about me at all. I just don't care about anything. I'm so miserable, I feel like dying. But don't worry, I won't; I'm too chicken to do it."

Sighing deeply, Stacy said, "I don't feel well. I can't understand it. Whatever I do for Rob, he lashes out at me." Stacy's body caved in as she said, "I can hardly drag myself out of bed, but I still cook his favorite foods, pick up after him, and most of all, I stay home and wait for him. I never know when to expect him. He gambles, you know, so sometimes I'm up all night waiting for him. If I'm asleep, he's furious. He wants his woman to wait up for him."

Rob was draining all of her inner strength, and to top it off, she was his willing accomplice. So many selfless women siphon off their own needs and desires to meet the needs and desires of others. Many of us know better, but it doesn't always matter.

Serotonin was locked in the synapse between neurons, so the receiving neuron could not pick it up to activate the specific serotonin receptor. This problem in neurotransmitter transmission had hampered the working order of her brain. "It's hard not to feel his despair. Like I told you, he's been losing at the tables, and I feel sorry for him. So when he lets it out at me, I try to look the other way."

"How does he 'let it out at you'?" I inquired.

In a monotone voice, she said, "He yells, pushes me around, and if I say anything in my defense, he hits me."

Like many women who live with domestic violence,

Stacy minimized the abuse. And like many victims, she assumed the blame for her partner's offenses: "I think you've got it wrong. It's not like he hits me hard. It's not like he ever broke any bones, just bruises. But that's only if I don't do what he wants. I've cried and apologized a lot. I keep saying I'm sorry and that I love him over and over. But he won't hear it. He threatened to belt me one if I didn't stop crying."

"Why do you take his abusive behavior? What's in it for you?" I asked.

Stacy had all the answers: "I want to make him happy. I want to make him feel powerful; he's my man. All hell breaks loose when he loses at the tables. I know what a loser feels like. And I feel sorry for him. So I try to make him feel like more of a man."

Stacy revealed that she felt powerless, weak, and stupid. Unable to help Rob, she felt even more inept. She wanted him to stop gambling, but as she said, "Winning at the tables is the greatest high, almost as good as cocaine." But the low is even worse than the cocaine crash. Rob goes into a tailspin and collapses. With their mirror neurons on a one-way street, Stacy resonated with Rob, but unfortunately, his gambling-induced mood swings eclipsed his empathy for Stacy.

I helped Stacy to see how she was ceasing to exist in her own right by living in Rob's shadow. She said, "I'm tired of the roller coaster ride. I want him to change. I know he can succeed in anything he tries. I'm forever praising him, trying to build his self-esteem, and encouraging him to do something else. Rob's smart, he was a philosophy major in college, but he dropped out because his father died, and he had to work to support the family. He screams at me to get off his back. But I can't give up, so I try to gently suggest other professions. With his charm, he'd make a good luxury car salesman, a commodity broker, or even a hedge fund manager." Despite the futility of her endeavors, Stacy persisted in trying to fix Rob and not herself.

I suggested that her fixation with making a successful man out of Rob was perhaps a distraction from herself, that her preoccupation with his career and accomplishments have kept her too busy to work on her own. I tried to convince here that more of a bad thing may make everything worse. Like many women in all walks of life, Stacy dreamed the impossible dream: "Rob says he loves me, so I can't give up the hope that, if he loves me, he'll change."

Love is a powerful force, but it's not powerful enough to change someone who doesn't want to change. No one is powerful enough to change someone else by coercion, let alone a woman who feels powerless. The more suggestions you offer, the more your partner will resent you and insult you. The more you try to build his self-esteem, the more he will dump on yours. With your self-esteem in the toilet, you're hardly in a position to save your partner from himself. Instead, you should focus on saving you.

I shared these ideas with Stacy, and her tone changed: "It's not like I get nothing out of this. When Rob's winning, we have the greatest sex, and I feel desirable. I feel in charge, that I'm powerful."

"Does Rob abuse his power?" I asked.

"The truth is that sex sometimes gets rough. Rob's passionate, and he gets carried away. Sometimes my head says it's not good for me, that it's humiliating and dangerous, but I can't stop. His hands on my neck choking me, his belt on my ass stinging me, should bring alarm, but the strange thing is that it's the greatest thrill and excitement imaginable."

Stacy had moved from drugs that gave her a high, from a profession that was exciting and thrilling, to a new type of drug, a sadomasochistic relationship. She had changed her addiction, not her inner self. Intent on fixing him and not herself, Stacy was bent on controlling Rob. This was yet another instance of the dynamic of control that went back and forth between Stacy and Rob.

Stacy and Rob came to a later session together. In therapy, Rob said to me, "I'm so happy to meet you. I've heard so much about you." Then he lowered his eyes modestly. "I'd bet you heard a lot about me. Stacy must've told you I was a monster. She's got it all wrong. I'm a gentle, generous, and good man. I don't know what she wants."

"I want you to stop gambling," said Stacy forthrightly.

Rob bellowed, "She tries to control me and I hate that! No one's gonna tell me what to do with my life."

In reality, Rob controlled everything about Stacy: her clothes, her friends, her activities. When she tried to

object, he tightened his grip on her, and she cried piti-
fully. His uncaring response was to tell her to stop crying
because he hated it.

Rob admitted in session that he felt horrible. He whis-
pered, "I feel helpless, hopeless, and powerless."

Stacy ventured, "Don't you see that when you feel terrible, so do I?"

Rob spat out these words: "That gets me so angry. I'm
not responsible for your feelings; only you are. Get a life,
Stacy! Get a life of your own!"

But Stacy continued to play her losing hand: "I feel
what you feel. I understand you. Don't push me away."

Rob responded, "You don't really know how I feel. Your
father never beat you, broke your bones and your spirit.
Your mother never fled your father and abandoned you
as a young child. So you can't possibly feel what I feel or
understand me. I feel alone." Tears welled up in Rob.

Stacy spoke softly: "I want to be your partner, Rob, but
I also want to be respected."

"And I love you and want to respect you," Rob said.

When asked if he was willing to work on the relationship, Rob said, "That's why I'm here. I love her, and I'm
afraid to be alone."

Stacy's mirror neurons were resonating with Rob's. She
said, "I'm afraid to be on my own also. My mother never
abandoned me physically, but she did emotionally. She was
trapped in a life of despair. My father was a drug addict,
and my mother was not the love of his life; the drugs were.

No matter how hard she tried to get him off the drugs, his addiction took his life. Hers went with him. She never got over it. I don't want to end up like my mother. But I see myself turning into her."

"Does any of this sound familiar?" I inquired.

Stacy answered: "All too familiar—I know I need my independence and autonomy. I'm beginning to see that I feed into this interaction. I've allowed Rob to stifle me, control me, and seduce me into a sadomasochistic relationship. I want to change myself."

"I'm so sorry that I hurt you. I got carried away, but I also want to change and make you happy," Rob pleaded.

Stacy asked the age-old question: "Can we really change? I feel like our problems are so deeply ingrained that it's impossible."

I tried to help Stacy and Rob have faith in themselves. They had both been reliving their old childhood trauma that was stamped deeper and deeper into their neural pathways. So, change may have seemed impossible for them, but it wasn't. It's amazing how adaptable the brain is, and how it can change. Rob and Stacy's new experiences and changed interactions helped them heal from the old trauma and realign their neural pathways.

With resolve and determination, Stacy and Rob began on a journey of relationship repair. They both realized that their unequal power relationship was hurting them. Stacy became aware that she was so dependent on Rob that she did everything to please him, to fix him, to save him, to cave into him—all so that he would love her and never leave her. She decided to change that dynamic, to fix and save herself. She is intent on feeling more powerful as a result of her own efforts and not by living vicariously through Rob's power.

As for Rob, he recognized how his childhood of abuse and abandonment left him feeling powerless. His need to gain power drove him to gamble and to control Stacy. A fast study, Rob was cooperative; his determination to change to fix the relationship helped him find new ways to gain power. Putting his pride aside, Rob took an entry-level job in commodities trading, where he is making great strides. His success is helping his self-esteem. More stable than gambling, the commodities field is also about risk taking. As a result, Rob still gets his kicks, but he does not get carried away like he did before.

Stacy has joined a group of women survivors of domestic violence, many of whom had substance abuse problems. Amazed that the women validated her opinions, empathized with her feelings of deep shame, and shared their inner worlds with her, she began to have faith that she was a worthwhile, intelligent, kind, and caring woman. Now she is savoring her strengths and facing her faults. As for her addiction, she is learning to replace her drug highs with pole dancing and jazz dance classes at the gym. Her new job as a fourth-grade teacher is satisfying and helping her to feel more independent. As she gains respect for her own strengths and values her independence, her mirror neurons reflect those feelings to Rob, who is gaining respect for her and valuing her more.

Stacy and Rob worked together on the communication exercises presented in this book, which they tried to do with reciprocity and mutuality. Forgiving Rob was essential for Stacy to let go of the past and live in the present, with hopes for a brighter future. Stacy's problem before was that she empathized too much with Rob. Now that she has experienced healthier relationships, she can empathize with him and stay put in her own shoes.

When Stacy saw that Rob was truly remorseful, with deep guilt, she was able to forgive him. He went to great lengths to make amends, which helped, and when she tackled her own demons, her humility helped even more. To top it off, their sexual relationship has moved from an abusive one to a loving but still lustful one.

Stacy and Rob have embarked on a new life path together, with new careers and new attitudes about equal power in their relationship. As their behavior and interactions change, so does their brain chemistry. Their mirror neurons activate neurons in the serotonin- and GABA-producing systems, so they feel happier and less anxious. Other brain chemicals that are released include oxytocin and vasopressin, which ensure trust, loyalty, devotion, and intimacy, along with testosterone and estrogen for romance and sex. During lovemaking, the surge of dopamine, norepinephrine, endogenous opioid peptides that resemble morphine, and nitric oxide provides the couple with euphoria, pleasure, love, and lust.

As you read the stories in this book, do you connect with the plights of the women? If your own relationship reminds you of aspects of their unequal dynamics, you may identify with the women's feelings. Let your feelings and thoughts flow freely, and see where they take you. They may wander along a string of associated memories. Follow the string for a glimpse of the scripts you wrote in childhood. Your mirror neurons will trigger the old family scripts and shine a bright light on them. Look at them clearly, so you can extricate them from your brain. As you reclaim your independent, autonomous self, you will start changing the dynamic of your relationship. In the process of creating deep inner change, you will rewire your brain and revise your relationship.

Chapter 8

Negative Fortune-Telling

Negative fortune-telling is the name I give to the unconscious process by which mirror neurons connect us in hurtful self-fulfilling prophesies. In a way, it's simple: you deny unwanted aspects of your character and wind up finding them in your partner. Is it black magic? Not really. In this chapter, I'll reveal the trick.

At an unconscious level, you may reject aspects of your character that you find unacceptable and start to look for them in your partner. This is "negative prediction." Mirror neurons reflect your suspicions of your partner to him or her. They also trigger your emotional and nonverbal communication, which may provoke him into acting out those onerous traits. Sure enough, then, your partner makes your suspicious belief come true.

In psychoanalytic circles, this unconscious process is known as projective identification.[67] In this process, you unconsciously project something you hate about yourself onto another person. Mirror neurons reflect your projection to your partner, and he identifies with it and acts it out. A more recent explanation of projective identification focuses on an interaction in which you unconsciously expect negative characteristics in your partner—that which you have unconsciously denied about yourself—and relate to him in such a way that he fulfills your prophesy.[68]

Tina is an example of a negative fortune-teller. She had found the perfect partner in Bert, a mild, reserved man. Proper and often bored and depressed, Tina secretly wished that she were a more frivolous, sexy, exciting, bold woman. She disdained other women who were like that and denied her own wishes, which remained hidden in her unconscious mind. Unwittingly, Tina had disconnected from her fun-loving side. She suspected that underneath Bert's proper front was a sexy, fun-loving guy. With the help of mirror neurons, he connected to her projection: her suspicions of his hidden character. At the same time, Tina's mirror neurons triggered provocative behavior and emotions aimed at Bert. She angrily accused him of harboring a secret dark side, of really wanting to let loose, curse, and race a motorcycle. Her provocations resulted in Bert's losing control, drinking up a storm, cursing, and purchasing a motorcycle. And so Bert fulfilled Tina's negative prophecy.

Before we look at what more goes on inside the brain, let's go back to the discovery of mirror neurons, which we learned about in chapter 1, to shed some light on this uncanny process.

Remember how monkeys were able to infer what the experimenter was about to do without seeing the action? The monkeys were able to make a mental representation of what they expected the experimenter to do. And that's because mirror neurons linked the monkey and experimenter in the same internal situation. In intimate relationships, humans also expect our intimate partners to behave in certain ways. And when a relationship is frayed, we expect negative behaviors from our partners. Such was the case with Christine and Ethan.

Raised by strict parents, Christine eschewed her mischievous, spiteful side and learned to behave like a good little girl. She grew up into a self-righteous, moralizing woman. What she really hated about herself was her sneaky, mean streak, so she disowned those traits and buried them in her unconscious mind. Exactly what happened to those traits? She found them in Ethan.

Intent on appearing aboveboard and kind, Christine was unconsciously conflicted. What to do about her hidden cruel traits? That's easy: unconsciously, she set up expectations for Ethan to act out his devious, cruel, underhanded traits.

By denying her sneaky, mean streak that Christine abhorred in herself, that streak remained latent in her unconscious mind. Mirror neurons between her and Ethan connected to those unconscious traits and triggered verbal and nonverbal communication that provoked Ethan to act in a devious, underhanded, mean way toward her.

In a saccharin voice, Christine accused Ethan repeatedly of what she secretly wanted to do—sneak out to drink with buddies, insult her, cut her off emotionally, and lie to her. Fearing her disdain, Ethan did in fact lie about things she would disapprove of. As for the cruel things, he lost his cool and called her uptight, prissy, sexless, and a no-good phony. To top it off, he pronounced that he'd had it with her and stormed out to meet with some of his drinking buddies.

Precisely because no one knew better than Christine quite how to push Ethan's buttons, the result was that Ethan fulfilled Christine's prophecy. Just as she expected, Christine was the decent, sweet angel, and Ethan was the immoral, cruel devil.

A negative fortune-teller operates behind the scenes. Let's say that you're the negative fortune-teller. No doubt, you possess positive sides and negative sides. But you may have a problem owning both sides because you want to see yourself in a certain favorable light. At an unconscious level, you disown your negative side and find it in your partner.

Aside from accepting all sides of yourself, another unconscious motivation of negative fortune-telling is that you can't accept the differences between your partner and you. For example, in a good relationship, your insecurities and your partner's self-assuredness complement each other. When you reject those differences, interlocking mirror neurons unconsciously wreak havoc with them;

rather than enriching both of you, the differences divide you into separate spheres.

Instead of mirror neurons reflecting complementary traits back and forth, polarized differences become even more disparate. The result is two opposite people. For example, if you can't stand your greedy, social-climbing side, you reject it and provoke your partner to act out those traits: your mirror neurons connect to your partner's actions, and you begin to live vicariously through, for example, your avaricious, social-climbing partner. Unfortunately, love and romance—which involve mutuality, reciprocity, and equal power—are on the rocks.

When love was fresh, those differences likely attracted you to your partner. You felt enhanced by the differences between the two of you. That's because there was flexibility in the relationship back then. Although you did not share all the same interests, you still had some things in common, so the differences worked for you. That was then, and this is now. Now, differences between your partner and you have become rigidly embedded, and it feels like you both are in different worlds.

The result? You feel despair. Your partner is your polar opposite, and there's no longer a meeting of minds, no give-and-take, no empathy, no emotional attunement. Not only that, but by unconsciously denying your unwanted traits and provoking your partner to act them out, you only deplete yourself. For example, we all need our aggressive, tough sides so that we can assert ourselves and stand up for ourselves; that way we feel enriched. When we disconnect from those qualities, we feel diminished. Nevertheless, many of us engage in negative fortune-telling.

What's the motivation to do so? To live up to an idealized, perfect, sense of ourselves. But, of course, human beings are not all good or all bad. We are not thoroughly aggressive or thoroughly passive, totally lively or totally dull, exclusively generous or exclusively greedy, full of pride or full of shame. With a healthy sense of self-worth, you can look inward and see not only your partner's negative characteristics but your own as well. In the process, you can begin to own your own hateful sides along with your cherished ones.

Unfortunately, many people can't own the bad along with the good. So much of their self-worth depends on how they'd *like to* see themselves, or an idealized false self, rather than who they *truly are*, or a true self. At an unconscious level, these people deny their negative traits and pretend to be perfect. In a sense they are fake, not authentic, people.

An example of this type of interaction is that of Diana and Matt. A virtuous, self-righteous, loyal wife, Diana more than noticed her handsome neighbor, Allen. The idea of having an affair with Allen crossed her mind, but before it took hold, she disconnected from her thoughts of cheating and relegated them to her unconscious mind. Diana accused her husband Matt of cheating, which he vehemently denied. Her continued badgering over numerous unfounded suspicions and her pronouncement that she no longer respected or liked him pushed Matt right into the arms of another woman. So, Diana's beliefs came true: Matt started cheating, and she remained the betrayed, loyal wife.

As with most negative attitudes and values, rejecting the sides of yourself that you detest is something you learned to do in your childhood. Was your mother strict, solemn, and steely at home, only to turn into a sweet, refined, gentle person when out with other people? If so, your mother likely wasn't accepting all sides of herself, and she was putting up a false front when out and the true self at home. Is this something you do, also? Maybe you put up a front of toughness at work and give in to your partner's unreasonable demands at home, or maybe you're all sweetness and light with the girls but bitter and scowling at home.

Then there's another old pattern of relating that may be playing out. This one features parents who disconnected from their hateful sides and pretended they were perfect but provoked each other to act out their very own imperfections.

For example, Gina's mother, Carmen, held herself up as kind, easygoing, flexible, and caring; her father, Sal, was hot tempered, rigid, and aggressive. Dig a little deeper, and we can unearth just how Carmen provoked Sal into losing it. A loving woman, Carmen was also overly permissive and unable to make decisions. Detesting strict, unreasonable parenting, Carmen unconsciously renounced her authoritative side and, unwittingly, coerced Sal into taking the reins. But there are two sides to any dynamic, and there may have been another side to all of this. In this case, Sal's overbearing, strict personality prompted Carmen to compensate with permissive, passive ways with her children. And so their differences were polarized.

Do you identify with either of these parents? There may be a different version that played out in your childhood. If so, those old family dynamics were seared into your unconscious mind so that you cringe when you think you're turning into your parent. You may even think you have married your parent.

We've just looked at the self-fulfilling prophesies that people create and how those interactions shape our intimate relationships in adulthood. Remember that in part 1, we discussed the interconnections of mirror neuron systems with other neuronal systems that activate memories and emotions. As such, if the dynamic of self-fulfilling prophesies held sway in your childhood, your unwanted sides may have been relegated to your unconscious memory. Mirror neurons may trigger this old dynamic so that now you renounce your less-than-stellar sides—aggression, meanness, greed, envy, shame, disloyalty, cowardice, or whatever else you may see as hateful. If so, you unconsciously provoke those characteristics in your partner. You deftly pull the aspects of yourself that you hate out of your partner's hat. If this is a dynamic playing out now in your relationship, then your mirror neurons have interlocked

your partner and you in a self-fulfilling prophecy, and the
relationship will slide downward.

Not only is your relationship in trouble, but this pattern of relating undermines your sense of self. Finding your unwanted sides in your partner and insisting that he change is tantamount to losing your own inner strength. The change I describe in the following sections is unconscious and at a deep, neural level; it is not conscious coercion or manipulation of your partner. And that's because you can't consciously make someone change: it takes a change in you and in the interaction for your partner to make some changes. If you have a fantasy that you can fix him, it's futile. You only waste your energy and strength in this endeavor. Not only that, but in doing so, you unwittingly transfer your power to him and render yourself powerless.

To rectify this sorry state of affairs, when you begin to accept and even embrace all of you—the bad along with the good, the toughness along with the tenderness, the aggression along with the cooperation—you will be transformed to a more whole, powerful woman. Your pattern of relating will stem from a solid foundation. You will then feel confident to act forthrightly, assertively, and competently. As you take back your power, mirror neurons will reflect those changes to your partner, so that he will change how he relates to you.

Here's how you can extricate yourself from this knotty dynamic.

FIVE STEPS TO TRANSFORMATION

1. Identify the Traits You Can't Stand in Your Partner

How do you feel when you think about the traits you can't stand in your partner? Are you angry, disappointed, sad, anxious, or fearful? For example, you may feel angry and impatient with your partner who does not, in your opinion, work hard enough to achieve. You may even believe or tell him that he's lazy. In contrast, maybe you hate his competitive, single-minded side. That's just one scenario of the many that may be playing out.

2. Assess the Possibility That These Traits Are Hidden in You

Remember that the traits we hate in ourselves—the ones hidden inside of us—are the traits we hate in our partners. Let's suppose your partner's laziness is maddening. Examine yourself. What do you do when things go awry in your career or at home? Do you sulk, pull the covers over you, pretend it's not a big deal? Or do you go into action to change things? Similarly, if you hate your partner's audacious chutzpah, are you afraid to show yours? Haul out your gutsy, daring side from hiding and take bold actions. That means you go after exactly what you want.

A patient of mine is an example of this. She was furious with her partner's laziness and kept pushing him to get certified as a personal trainer. It turned out that she had

never received her certification as a nutritionist, and her
practice was in trouble. Once she saw where that hated
laziness lay—inside of her—she went into action and
began studying to take her certification test. She focused
on correcting her own shortcoming and not her partner's.
With matching mirror neurons, her self-focus and drive
unconsciously prompted him to change. Without being
coerced by her, he went back to school to pursue a career
as a gourmet chef, which he had always wanted.

3. Practice the Keys from Earlier Chapters

With internal feelings of power, good communication
skills, empathy, and the ability to forgive, you may just
get what you want. For example, in interactions with your
partner, if you show more of your introspective, quiet
sides, your partner may show more of his extroverted,
lively sides. Or if you are the selfless giver, try asking more
of him—he may be more generous and giving. No longer
polarized, the two of you can share differences that were
rigidly ingrained in your separate brains.

4. Get Real and Take Responsibility for Your Role in the Dynamic

Get in touch with times when you, unwittingly, provoked
your partner into hurtful actions. For example, do you
expect your partner to be inattentive and neglectful, and

does he always live up to that expectation? Now is the time to examine yourself so that you can see that, rather than participating or standing up for yourself, you quietly withdraw. No one knows your partner quite like you do. Aware that he is an ambitious, busy guy, when you push his buttons by disappearing from his sight, he will react by ignoring you. So, your behavior may have prompted this not-so-magical phenomenon.

If you're dealing with a possessive and jealous partner, think about how you play into it. Do you flirt with other men in front of your partner? If so, can you change your behavior? Then again, if your partner is controlling, you may submit too quickly or feign helplessness. Try gently confronting him, standing up for yourself, and beginning to take back your power. As you change, you will feel more fulfilled, and mirror neurons will link both of you in a healthier dynamic.

5. Develop a Strong Sense of Self

It takes a strong sense of self to step back from this interaction of negative fortune-telling and to take responsibility for things you hate about yourself. Let's review some of the ways you can empower yourself. Take stock of your assets and accomplishments, acknowledge your shortcomings, and transform them to strengths. If you are hiding your aggression, join a group of active, assertive women who can act as role models. Start the process of

self-care: join an exercise program, and focus on your diet
and your physical well-being. As you begin to feel more
powerful internally, you can create change in yourself and
in your relationship.

Meet Maxine and Arlen, locked in a dynamic of negative
fortune-telling that has led to a loveless relationship. But
their story shows how to transform links of pain to links
of love.

♡ The fit and the feckless

Lean of midriff, long of leg, Maxine was in amazing shape.
A pinstriped suit never looked so seductive, nor did a hard-
working, hard-nosed, fifty-two-year-old woman. Modesty
was not important to her: indeed, her low-cut neckline
had a close encounter with her hemline.

"My life's so pressured and stressful, and his is so easy.
He's too lazy to get a job and spends his time playing his
stupid guitar. How can I love him?" She had turned shrill.

Undisciplined rolls of flab strained at Arlen's seams as
a button popped. "But I need you, Maxine. I love you,
baby," he pleaded.

Maxine zinged, "Stop sniveling. I hate needy, clingy
people."

Arlen said softly, "Maybe if you were more supportive
and less demanding, I'd try harder."

"Stop blaming me for your incompetence and laziness!" Maxine snapped.

Maxine and Arlen were connected by mirror neurons. Maxine acted out her unsavory side and Arlen lived vicariously through his brazen, ball-busting wife. In doing so, he disowned his own tough side. Arlen enjoyed the financial benefits of Maxine's high salary. He had sold his soul and his aggressive nature for an easy ride. As a "kept" man, Arlen could pretend he was worthy and special. What a powerful position for a powerless man!

When Arlen goofed off and feigned tenderness, Maxine was cast as the tough go-getter. Arlen disowned his independent, assertive, industrious side and played the dependent, passive, fun-loving, lackadaisical reactor. In turn, Maxine disowned her helpless, easygoing, feckless side and played the independent, aggressive, serious-minded actor. Unwittingly, they provoked each other to play out these rejected, discordant sides of their separate characters. Living vicariously through each other, their mirror neurons linked them in misery.

In therapy, we looked at Maxine and Arlen's childhoods. Maxine's father, a shiftless gambler, had landed in jail and left her mother to fend for herself. With four young children to feed and no education, Maxine's mother left the house early in the morning to clean houses, only to return late at night to clean her own. Love and tenderness took a backseat to tough, gritty, no-nonsense perseverance. No wonder Maxine's independence was shaped early on. Fearing a fate like her mother's, Maxine had used her skills to better her life. The oldest child, she baby-sat, disciplined, and reprimanded her younger siblings. In her marriage to Arlen, she unconsciously replicated the old childhood dynamic that featured her as the house mother.

A hidden part of Maxine envied Arlen's relaxed, care-free, childlike life. She secretly longed to be pampered, to check her brain at the door and surrender to fun, but she disowned those traits for fear that they'd overtake her. Instead, she believed Arlen was an irresponsible child; her insulting, demeaning behavior enfeebled him, and by becoming spineless, he fulfilled her negative expectations, her fortune-telling. The fitter and abler that Maxine became, the more feckless and ineffective Arlen became. Living vicariously through Arlen, she had almost everything, except an authentic self and a loving relationship.

Arlen's childhood starred a passive mother and a critical, hard-hearted father who took out his wrath on Arlen and his mother. The more his father punished Arlen, the more he berated him, the more he tried to make a tough man out of him, the more Arlen retreated and cowered. Fearing that his own aggression would turn him into his father, Arlen identified with his powerless mother. The old script taught him to disavow his tough, gritty sides; the ground seemed safer that way. And because the part of him that he disowned was precisely what sprouted in Maxine, mirror neurons entwined them, allowing him to live vicariously through her.

Communicating their needs to each other in ways to get them met went by the wayside, as did empathy and emotional attunement. Mirror neurons connected them in nasty insults, attacks, and defensiveness. In one therapy session, we addressed the issue of Maxine's enabling Arlen. When Maxine plays the active role, Arlen plays the passive one—and when Arlen plays the passive role, Maxine plays the active one.

Maxine took stock of the situation: "Yup, I think I'm enabling him. He called me at work and told me he was off to Disneyland with our daughter, Lisa, and her baby. She's just like him, operating at a whim, neither of them plans ahead. No reservations, no hotel, his guitar and a newborn baby in tow. Guess who paid for it? I did. That's been the story of our marriage: I slave the hours away and he plays the hours away."

Arlen attacked back: "That's not the whole story. You may be a money-making machine, but I don't want to live with a well-calibrated machine. I want a wife. If you allowed yourself to loosen up and go with the flow, you may even get to like it. Not every move needs a blueprint, nor is *spontaneity* a dirty word."

Maxine reprimanded Arlen further: "Life is serious, not fun. If you got more serious and didn't waste so much time, we'd be in better shape."

One reprimand begets another. Arlen responded: "We'd also be in better shape if you were more modest. I hate how you parade around half naked at work. It's scandalous."

Absorbing the blow, Maxine asked, "What's scandalous about looking hot? I'm an attorney in the film industry; I can't dress priggish. You don't seem to mind the lucrative contacts I sign."

And so it went on: attacks, defense, more attacks, and more defense and more hurt. Here's how the dynamic moved from links of pain to links of love. In therapy, I encouraged Maxine to let her guard down and surrender to her softer sides. She even toyed with the idea of reclaiming her disowned desires for a less structured, more relaxed life: a mindless TV show, a topping of whipped cream, a spontaneous quickie. Her boundless imagination was itching to break through the self-imposed barriers of restraint.

Slowly, she is giving in to some of her rejected desires and is able to relax, play, and surrender to her footloose and fancy-free sides. She actually overslept one day, called in sick, and read a popular novel. As she loosens her reins, Arlen is beginning to tighten his grip on his own.

Just as Maxine's sense of herself is expanding to include some typically feminine traits that she rejected in herself, Arlen's sense of himself is expanding to include some typically masculine traits. He is less afraid of his aggressive, powerful sides. The more he takes action, the more Maxine respects him and the more confidence he gains. His diet is not exactly under control and a button or two may still pop at his middle, but Maxine is more tolerant of her own indulgences and, in turn, of Arlen's.

In therapy, Maxine and Arlen were able to get in touch

with the sides of themselves they had disconnected from and to see how they appeared in the other person. By uncovering some of the pain from their early years, they learned that, although their responses helped them adapt in childhood, things are different now. That insight helped them gain compassion for themselves and for each other. The work of reclaiming the parts of themselves that they have disowned is ongoing.

Maxine is learning how to empathize with her own dilemma and seeing how she deprived herself from the simpler pleasures of life—a response to her difficult childhood that became imprinted in her brain. In therapy, she has learned that her brain is plastic, which inspired her determination to make changes in her life. Once she recognized the effects of her old family relationship on her personality and her interaction with Arlen, she became more trusting and less fearful of her vulnerabilities. Now, instead of attacking Arlen, she stops and thinks about the effect on him, softens her tone of voice, and relaxes her body language. In a tender voice, she tells Arlen, "I strained my back today. A massage would feel so good." At last, Arlen could step up to the plate and take care of his wife.

The mirror neurons that linked Maxine and Arlen in a system of interacting selves are busy lining up new styles of relating. Instead of disowning unwanted parts of themselves and finding them in the other person, the couple is learning to acknowledge and accept those traits as part of their own selves. And instead of depleting themselves by projecting those parts they dislike onto their partners, each partner, hopefully, is feeling more whole.

Maxine and Arlen had become entangled in the deadly dynamic of negative fortune-telling in their own way. Other couples, like Grace and Darren, play out this dynamic in other ways.

♡ Sweet and Sorry Sides

Darren sauntered into a therapy session with Grace trailing behind. Sighing deeply, Grace sputtered, "I…I…I'm exhausted. I can't talk. We had a houseful of guests. Darren's sister and brother-in-law and their five wild kids dropped in unannounced. Even though I was nursing a cold, I was out in the pouring rain grocery shopping and buying presents for the children. That's not easy. They're fussy eaters, one's a vegetarian, another has food allergies, and they all like different things. Anyhow, I made sure everyone got exactly what they liked."

"You always do too much and you get exhausted. That's nothing new. You just like complaining," Darren said while rolling his eyes.

Grace looked frustrated. "See how he insults me? I do things for others because I'm a good, kind person. It's just who I am. I'm not like him."

Darren expressed his discomfort: "You're not like me, all right. I'm not a martyr like you. No one asked you to do all that."

"Maybe if you helped, if you lifted a finger, I wouldn't have to be such a martyr," Grace retorted.

Darren protested, "Whenever I try to help, you criticize how I do things, so I don't bother anymore."

"That's not true. I'm not a critical person. It's just that you don't know how to do anything in the kitchen. It's not your fault, sweetheart. Your old-fashioned mother idolized you and did everything for you."

"I hate when you criticize my mother!" Darren shouted.

Grace reprimanded him: "Stop shouting at me. You twist everything around. I'm not criticizing her."

"Who're you kidding?" Darren snapped back.

Bypassing the road to self-awareness, Grace took the more traveled road of denial: "It's not like I don't work. There's a shortage of nurses at the hospital, and I'm on my feet running from patient to patient all day. Between back-breaking work on the job and then at home, I'm totally stressed out." Rubbing her temples, she groaned, "I'm getting another migraine."

Darren bellowed, "There she goes again, the self-sacrificing angel of mercy! I make plenty of money, so she doesn't have to work."

Grace winced and said, "See how heartless and selfish he is? He knows I'm in pain, but he's too busy defending himself to pay any attention to me. It's not the first time. Last month, I had the flu and was shivering on the sofa. He didn't get up to help me; instead, he told our son to get me a cold towel."

"I had a hard day at work, and I had to lie down," Darren said.

"Do you believe this? The reason I help people is because I'm a giver, not like you."

"There she goes again. I work my butt off to give you and the kids everything you want. You have no problems spending money and racking up huge credit card bills." Darren's angry protest was turning his ruddy complexion to purple.

Grace composed herself and pointed to her well-worn jeans and cotton shirt. "In case you didn't notice, these are not exactly Armani. I don't spend money on me; it's for you and the kids and your family with their five kids. Not only was last weekend expensive; it wiped me out. You not only didn't help out; you were busy doing your thing all day Saturday."

Unruffled, Darren defended himself: "You know, I'm under pressure at work all week, and I need Saturdays to wind down. I hate that you're always bitching about me."

Grace responded, "He's always angry with me. I hate it."

I suggested that perhaps what they hated in each other was what they hated about themselves. Grace may hate what she perceived as Darren's selfishness, and Darren may hate what he perceived as Grace's self-sacrificing martyrdom. But Grace was not ready to relinquish her role as the all-suffering angel. In Grace's emotional state, accepting that she had a self-serving side would be cataclysmic, so she hung on to her martyrdom for dear life. Their litany of bitter complaints continued, and so did the excuses.

To extricate themselves from this dynamic, in the following sessions, Grace and Darren began to get in touch with the sides of themselves that they hated and had disconnected from. A review of their respective family dynamics illuminated the roots of their interaction with each other.

Grace's sickly mother suffered her first heart attack at age forty. A stroke a few years later left her with a limp, a speech impediment, and a dependency on caretakers. Bittersweet memories of a kind, loving, selfless mom and an aloof, self-centered father had drifted into Grace's brain and become entrenched. She recalled her father as a healthy, powerful, and heartless man. Her father had disowned his own weakness and could not tolerate it in others. Strength was the greatest good in her household. Her father abandoned his wife to pursue his own interests, and the role of caretaker to her mother and herself fell to ten-year-old Grace. Although play took a backseat to duty, acting as a caretaker conferred inordinate power on Grace. Her father often complimented her independent, stalwart nature. The seeds of her self-sacrificing personality were planted.

As an adult, Grace disowned her self-serving, needy parts and held tight to her ideal image of a powerful, self-sufficient giver. Miraculously, she found her disowned parts in Darren. His needs came ahead of hers. Whenever he failed to act out those parts she had disowned, she provoked him into acting them out. Often she sabotaged any help or caring he offered and maintained her strong position of needing no one.

Darren's childhood relationships revealed a downtrodden mother and a hard-drinking, not hard-working, father. Not only were material needs rationed, the meeting of emotional needs was also in short supply. His father took every opportunity to rant, rave, and berate his wife. The house was never clean enough, his socks were never in the right drawer, the stew was too thick, and the spaghetti too thin. The belt, the fist, or the shoe stung many of the children's bodies and maimed their spirits.

Busy stretching food to feed her family, busy keeping the house and her children clean, Darren's mother's energy was low. Protecting her children from their father's abuses took more energy and strength than she could muster. The children learned to fend for themselves and fight for their share of the meager pickings. Grabbing for oneself was the greatest good. Darren's roots as a taker were well watered.

Vowing not to turn into his father, Darren disavowed alcohol and his angry, critical, self-centered sides. Identifying with his weak mother, who had sacrificed for her family, was not an option for success—and Darren wanted to succeed. It took a tough, competitive fighter to succeed in corporate America. Darren was a natural at work but not at home.

Recognizing the old family styles of interacting provided the opportunity for Darren and Grace to disentangle themselves and create change. As Grace became aware that her self-sacrifices were not entirely selfless, that there was something in it for her, things began to look up. The turning point was when Grace accepted her need for power and began to find other ways to boost her self-esteem.

As her self-serving, critical sides came out of hiding, Grace could more readily accept them in Darren. She also learned how she expected him to behave in a certain way and, unwittingly, coerced him to act out her expectations. Her negative fortune-telling had come true, but her life lacked fulfillment.

She decided to cut her work down to three days per week, to spend more time caring for herself, and to accept help from others. It was not as though Grace stopped caring for others, but by caring for herself, her motivations changed, as did her relationship with Darren.

It takes two to participate in the dynamics of negative fortune-telling, but it takes only one to begin to change the dynamic. As Grace grew and changed, so did Darren. His self-aware journey brought the sides of himself that he detested out into the open. He learned how his disdain for self-sacrifice was based in his disdain for his own self-sacrifice. In his corporate world, the most competitive, self-serving taker survives, whereas the selfless giver dies off. It was not as though Darren did not harbor kind, caring, uncritical, and unselfish sides; it was just that they signaled defeat, and so he unconsciously kept them submerged. He soon saw how they surfaced in Grace.

By trying on some of his kinder, gentler, considerate

sides, Darren found that he liked how they fit. Putting Grace first did not mean he would be trampled on. The more he helped her, the more he put a smile on her face and the more he valued his newfound manhood and his wife. Expressing his tender, unselfish sides did not destroy his tough, self-serving sides; it allowed Grace to share in both sides of the coin.

Grace learned how to elicit empathy from Darren and, without complaining, how to get her needs met. And sure enough, Darren felt empathy for Grace and, in a different sense, got his needs met also. Forgiveness for each other, emotional attunement, reciprocity, and mutuality were on the horizon.

Now that you've visited the stories of Maxine and Arlen, and Grace and Darren, it is time to reflect on these stories, surrender to your feelings, and allow your mirror neurons to resonate with those of some of the characters you just read about. What bubbles up? Do their dilemmas remind you of yours? Do other interactions come to mind? Do you see yourself or your partner in any of these scenarios? How about aspects of their personalities? Do their personalities inspire you to look at yours?

Let's review some of the keys to unlocking the brain from the negative fortune-telling style of relating. The first key issue is the influence of old family relationships on your current relationship. Take a hard look at how the relationship problem, troublesome as it is, is even more troubled when burdened by your old family interactions. In fact, the burden amounts to double trouble—your unhealthy family dynamics and your current problematic relationship—that can overwhelm you. Only by disentangling yourself from those old patterns of relating, by becoming aware of the impact of the past on the present, can you lighten the load to the point that you can rewire your brain. And only by rewiring the brain and bringing back love chemicals can you work directly on changing yourself and your relationship. Then you can make room for new interactions of shared traits.

The second key is to develop a strong sense of self. Once you work on self-empowerment, you will be in a better position to accept your negative traits and to stop blaming your partner for those traits. With a stronger sense of self, you can accept your limitations and, in turn, your partner's. Also, when your partner pushes your buttons, you will be able to recognize just how you are provoking him. With your free will and plastic brain, you can change your attitude and your behavior.

The third key is to communicate your needs when caught up in the negative fortune-telling dynamic. Anger is often a response to hurt. Rage is one of the best antidotes to depression, so when you feel hurt, you often strike out in anger. You complain, insult, attack, reject, defend yourself, and lose sight of how to get your needs met. Once you get in touch with your pain, with your sadness and feelings of helplessness, hopelessness, or depression, you can reach out to your partner in a gentler, kinder, more inviting way. You will be able to say, "I feel so sad about our fights" instead of "You always start the fights."

The fourth key is to be aware of how you lose sight of empathy when your brain is locked in the dynamic of negative fortune-telling. This self-fulfilling style of relating perpetuates itself, perniciously, by goading you to attack your partner and defend yourself. Feeling empathy for yourself entails reclaiming your renounced characteristics, feelings, and actions.

Once you recognize how you got here, through early relationships and social roles you identified with, you will be in a better place to feel compassion for yourself. Then the unwanted traits won't seem so despicable to you. By accepting the parts of yourself that you hate, you are freer to empathize with your partner. And then mirror neurons can link you to your partner in a fresh interaction of empathy and emotional attunement.

It takes an understanding of the role of negative fortune-telling in your relationship to get things going. With this insight, you can take steps to extricate the old negative fortune-telling from your brain. You can then make room for your mirror neurons to connect your partner and you in new positive ways of relating.

Along the way, serotonin and GABA will boost your positive moods, and vasopressin and oxytocin will bring you closer to your partner. What's more, dopamine and norepinephrine will immerse you both in exciting romantic pleasure. Your mirror neurons may even trigger the release of endogenous opioid peptides—which resemble morphine and nitric oxide—to heighten the euphoria. If so, you may find that sexual desire is making a comeback. As your sexual desire returns, you will become acquainted with the most erogenous zone in the body—the brain. The next chapter will inspire you to rekindle the flame and connect love and lust.

Chapter 9

Connecting Love and Lust: Rekindling the Flame of Desire

asking in the sunlight, Gigi and Omar, my fluffy Persian kitties, purred contentedly. Omar roused himself to gently lick and groom Gigi. Delighted, she upturned her face to accept. Attentive and loving, the happy couple basked in enchanted paradise.

Caught up in the magic of the moment, the sexual side of nature was suspended. But not for long. The unruly sexual side of nature refuses to be harnessed. Omar's love-play suddenly grew excitedly fierce and escalated in feverish bites. Swatting him with her paw, Gigi hissed and scampered away. He chased after her. No matter how sweet and caring Omar is, no matter how tender and gentle, no matter that he was neutered, Omar's sexual instincts lurked out of sight.

Adam and Emma were a couple with a similar problem. They cared deeply for each other and still loved each other. Although Adam desired Emma sexually, she had been neutered emotionally—his extramarital affair had placed Emma's sexual desire in the freezer.

"I want my wife back!" His overtures failed to thaw Emma's resolve.

Emma responded with disdain: "I haven't gone anywhere, not like you. You left me when you had the affair."

Adam said, "That was ten years ago! I've done everything to make it up to you."

"I know you have, and I've forgiven you for it. I care for you, I'm devoted to you, and I love you. I'm your best friend." Emma wasn't yielding, but her tone was gentler.

Adam matched her softness: "I know that, and I appreciate everything you do for me. And you're my best friend, but I want more. I want a lover."

"I want it, too, but I can't get that feeling back again," Emma whimpered.

Emma, like many people in long-term relationships, wanted to bring romance and sexual desire back into the relationship. Even when they are no longer in love with their partners, women persist in loving, caring for, and devoting themselves to their partners. Despite the trauma of betrayal or emotional and physical abuse, women still continue to care about their partners, even when the flame of sexual desire has snuffed out.

The case of Emma and Adam is a relationship fraught with traumatic events of adultery, but what about other long-term relationships? Do all seasoned relationships lose their sizzle over time? Not necessarily; there is hope. If you

are in one of those relationships where romance, passion
and lust have faded, this chapter will show you how to
bring it back.

Remember the high, that cloud-nine feeling, you felt
when you first fell in love? Your partner and you, like
many couples, may still love and care for each other,
and have a loyal and trustworthy relationship. Maybe
infidelity or abuse has not stained the relationship, but
misunderstandings, blame, criticism, control issues,
poor communication, or empathy failures have not
been resolved. The relationship then settles into one of
love—familiarity, friendship, shared interests, security,
comfort, devotion, commitment, caring. Gone is the
lust—excitement, spontaneity, novelty, romance, passion, sexual desire. Lust has been disconnected from
love, and the relationship limps along.

What is missing is the dopamine rush—the brain chemical that promotes ecstatic pleasure during excitement,
passion, spontaneity, eroticism—along with endogenous
opioids and testosterone, which enhance romance and
lust. Serotonin and GABA, the good-mood neurotransmitters, are also on hold. And it seems you can never bring
back that incredible erotic feeling. But you can.

No matter the rut you are in, no matter how dispirited
you feel, no matter how short the supply of good-mood
neurotransmitters and love-inducing brain chemicals, you
can change all of this. You can bring romance, passion,
and sexual desire back. You can reconnect love and lust.

First, it is important to understand the unconscious motivations for disconnecting lust from love. Often, it is either the fear of getting hurt again or the fear of losing your partner. If you surrendered to sexual desire along with devotion, to excitement along with comfort, to spontaneity along with familiarity, to passion along with security, to love along with lust, then you would have everything in one person. In the event that you experience trauma or lose your partner to illness, death, or separation, you would lose everything. So much to risk!

Sure enough, there is a way to protect yourself from hurt. Once you disconnect lust from love—a most ironic solution—you are less vulnerable. You no longer have that much to lose, and you feel safe. Through mirror neurons, you reflect chummy behavior and unromantic feelings to your partner.

Unfortunately, when you bring love to the foreground and push lust to the background, you squeeze the life out of the relationship and the electricity out of the neural circuits. You then have the steak without the sizzle. Meet Jane and Ian, a couple who succumbed to a humdrum, comfortable life with love, friendship, familiarity, and devotion. Placing excitement, spontaneity, passion, and eroticism on the back burner, they unwittingly snuffed the flame of desire.

"You'd think he was the woman in this relationship," Jane said smugly. "You get hurt so easily," she told him, "and you're always the victim."

Ian appealed to me: "I've no idea what she's talking about. She has a mouth like a drunken sailor, only she doesn't drink. She strikes out at me, curses, and carries on if I don't do things the way she likes. She needs to go to charm school. You think you're so funny, Jane. But what's not so funny is the way you attack me for everything. I didn't fix the roof the way you wanted it, the bushes weren't trimmed the way you wanted, the leaves weren't brushed off the front stoop. Everything I did wasn't good enough for you."

Jane became more humble. "I'm so sorry, darling, but I didn't insult you or berate you."

Ian retorted, "Really? What do you call telling me to 'forget it' when I wanted to make love to you? That's one big insult. Guess what? I forgot it. I no longer want to have sex with you."

Jane wailed, "Can't you see how hurtful you are? I'm trying so hard to pick myself up from the depths of despair after caring for my elderly parents. You have no empathy at all."

"I know that it was hard on you, but why'd you have to sacrifice me and yourself while you were caring for them? The stress and strain of your ordeal left no time for me. I was neglected." Ian's show of empathy quickly shifted to self-interest.

Jane nearly exploded: "Like I said, you have no empathy for me. That's painful enough, but you can't imagine the pain I feel that you don't want me sexually. "

"I can't change my feelings. You know I love you, and I care deeply for you. But I feel alone. You go off into your room and I go into mine, and we watch our own TV shows separately. We've gotten into this comfortable routine."

Jane and Ian were both retired, so they had created their own schedules, but those schedules never seemed to coincide.

Ian said, "There was a time when we were in sync with each other. We're both spiritual and liberal, and we love nature—we traveled all over the world. We snorkeled, sailed, fished, and made love on the beach." Their mirror neurons had matched up in these vital areas of an intimate relationship, but other aspects of intimacy had gone awry. But today, matching mirror neurons connected their depressed mood states.

Jane piped up: "Don't get me wrong. It's not that we're miserable. Actually, we feel comfortable, safe, and secure with each other. We don't cheat, gamble, do drugs, or drink excessively. Not only that, but we love each other."

I asked whether anger or resentment might underlie their habit of having separate rooms.

Ian jumped in: "Well, I'm angry with her, all right. She criticized and attacked me constantly, and then she rejected me sexually."

"I was so distraught about my parents that sex was the

last thing on my mind. I guess I let my frustration out on you. But now you're punishing me and holding sex back. That's so painful for me."

"I'm just not ready. I have to heal first," Ian said softly.

Once again, mirror neurons linked them in a similar goal as Jane grew more tender. "I guess I need more healing also."

We had previously worked on how Ian and Jane could savor their strengths and face their frailties, how they could communicate verbally and nonverbally. To facilitate further healing, we looked to their childhoods and found that childhood ghosts still haunted them.

Here was a couple whose mirror neurons had linked them in a multitude of attitudes, beliefs, and interests. But the most surprising commonality was their fear of abandonment. Jane's mother abandoned her early in life when she became sick with an undiagnosed illness. Eight years before the current therapy session, her mother was diagnosed with Alzheimer's, and Jane lost her again. Despite the stress and strain of caring for her ill mother, Jane did not seek solace elsewhere. Instead, she stayed glued to her mother until she finally died. Her fear of abandonment haunted her relationship with Ian.

Ian's fear of abandonment also stemmed from an old script with his parents. His father beat his older brother, who in turn beat Ian. Since Ian was much smaller and weaker than his brother, fighting was not an option, and so he fled. The old script of fleeing attack exacerbated his relationship with Jane so that, in his mind, she became the fearsome brother from whom he fled. Just as Ian could not please his father, he could not please Jane. His preoccupied mother was too busy to defend young Ian; in essence, she abandoned him.

That was then, and this is now. Jane and Ian had so much going for them—love, caring, shared history, interests, commitment. What they lacked was the life force of any relationship—excitement, adventure, spontaneity, romance, and sexual desire. With newfound insight and continued work to enhance self-esteem and communicate effectively, they were better able to resolve some of the disappointment, resentment, and hurt that had invaded their relationship.

Closer to reconnecting love and lust, Jane and Ian still needed more work on empathy and forgiveness. To arrive at forgiveness, we reviewed the three steps—empathy, repair, and humility.

Jane and Ian learned to step into each other's shoes so that matching mirror neurons reflected empathic feelings back and forth. Jane got in touch with her inner feelings of sadness, anxiety, and fear of abandonment, and she took the time to feel empathy for herself. She then explained to Ian how she felt—undesirable, unwomanly, depressed—when he rejected her sexually. Mirror neurons reflected Jane's feelings—ineptitude, unworthiness, and depression—so that Ian was able to experience them.

Rather than defending himself as he had in the past, Ian reached out to Jane to comfort her. By reading his verbal and nonverbal communication, Jane felt that he was sincerely remorseful and that he felt guilty. When Ian requested forgiveness, Jane immediately granted it.

It was then Ian's turn. As he proceeded to express his feelings of hurt, rejection, abandonment, and anger, he did so gingerly and with compassion. Jane was impressed and felt truly sorry that she had caused him such grief and despair. By empathizing with him, she could walk in his shoes. She asked him for forgiveness, which he granted her without hesitation.

With healing under way and empathy restored, Emma and Adam and Jane and Ian were ready to follow some of the exercises to help their mirror neurons drive them to lovemaking and lust. Are you ready?

Bringing lust back into a relationship takes a backseat to excavating past resentment, anger, disappointment, and pain from the brain. With tuned-up mirror neurons and renewed brain chemistry, you are now in a better place to practice the keys of bringing intimacy back—transforming old childhood ghosts to harmless ancestors, mobilizing your inner strength, communicating your needs verbally and nonverbally, and harnessing the healing power of empathy and forgiveness.

By removing stumbling blocks from your path, you pave the way for new, rich, and satisfying experiences. You have love, but what about lust? Can you have real intimacy in your relationship without the thrill of erotic experience? No!

The following sections show you how to trigger the power of brain chemistry to make room for a new relationship that connects love and lust in potent and intimate ways. There are four stages to lovemaking: the previews, the opening act, the main act, and the final act.

THE PREVIEWS
Fantasize

- Action begins in the mind, in the imagination. Research shows that imagination can change the brain and trigger the release of love-inducing brain chemicals. Remember when you were madly in love, when you could not take your hands off your partner? When you melted at the mere sight or sound of each other? When your body tingled with a waft of his aroma? When he undressed you with his voice, eyes, gestures, and body language? When holding his hand quickly led to sensuous passionate embraces? That's when lust was stronger than love.

- Visualize the scene—the where, when, and how—and relive those feelings. Were you on a deserted beach, in the woods, parked in a secluded spot, in a cozy bed-and-breakfast, on your sofa at home? Was it dawn, late morning, midday, afternoon, evening, or nighttime? How did he seduce you, or how did you seduce him? Was it mutual, spontaneous, and reciprocal? Mirror neurons were reflecting the magic of lust to your partner and you.

- Stay there in your imagination and let the experience wash over you. What are you feeling?

Take the Fantasy Further

- Imagine the soft light of dawn caressing your bodies and feel only sexual desire. Fantasize about a delightful romp in the afternoon in broad daylight or a romantic, candlelit dinner at home with lovemaking between courses. Bring to mind a hot weekend escape on a tropical island or in a lodge with snow-covered mountains in the background. Imagine that you return to a scene where you once made passionate love. Your fantasies should involve only you and your partner—no children, chores, or commitments.
- Whatever you imagine, it is important to remember the titillating effect of novelty, spontaneity, and excitement on sexual desire. Imagine bringing excitement into your relationship with new sexual positions and lovemaking in new places. If you've always made love in bed, imagine making love in a hot-air balloon, the shower, on a sunny beach.
- Make a mental picture of the verbal and sensual foreplay that has aroused your desire in the past and imagine prolonging that feeling before having sex.
- For a thrilling experience, change things around in your mind. If your partner always initiates foreplay, imagine that you are undressing him and beginning the action.

Or if you are silent before or during lovemaking, imagine yourself panting out loud or talking dirty to your partner. All is fair in love and lust.

THE OPENING ACT
Set the Stage

- Before you act on your sexual arousal—which can feel unsettling or even threatening—set the stage for the romantic drama. To create a safe distance from the sex act, send a steamy text, email, or phone call to your partner so that you can get the water warm before you take the plunge.

- In these indirect ways of communication, begin by expressing your innermost feelings, wishes, desires, fantasies, and intentions to your partner. His mirror neurons will reflect your feelings and actions.

- As you continue the dialogue, excitement will mount, so go for it. Forget modesty; be explicit and even raunchy. Tell your partner what you'd like him to do to you and what you'd like to do to him. His mirror neurons will reflect your lack of inhibition, and he may even top you with his free abandon. Make the anticipation sexy!

- Experience the thrill, excitement, and heightened emotions and sensuousness of anticipating lovemaking. With no holds barred, your partner will no doubt reciprocate or raise the level of excitement by revealing his own erotic ideas to you.

- At this point, you both feel a compelling sexual longing for each other. Stay with the experience and let it dig deep into your brain.

Behind the Scenes

Novelty is vital to successful lovemaking. You can set the scene for lovemaking in ways that you may have used in the past—soft music, candles, loving words, sensual touching and kissing—but there is nothing quite as exciting as a new experience. You may want to try tantric sex, an ancient Hindu practice that raises the sexual experience to a spiritual level. Here's a brief look at how your partner and you can practice some of the spiritual rituals of tantric sex:

- Light the room with two candles, which represent spiritual and sexual surrender. Play soft rhythmic, pulsating music that reflects the movements and emotions of foreplay and sex.
- Empty your mind. While naked, sit cross-legged opposite your partner and imagine the third eye—the spot a bit above where your eyebrows meet. The focus on your third eye disconnects you from distracting thoughts, anxieties, or bad memories and helps you stay in the moment.
- Bathing, which symbolizes preparing the temple of your body for a feast, is an essential tantric ritual. Lather your body well as you caress your curves and the erogenous zones. Luxuriate in the experience. Then, either don a silk robe or approach your partner nude.

The stage is set with the rituals behind the scenes in place. Now the action begins. Lay down the foundation for the main theme—the sex act. Let sensual and verbal foreplay linger. Coordinate your movements to the pulsating background music.

THE MAIN ACT

Surrender to the ecstatic feelings that surface from deep inside of you. Only then can you surrender fully to your partner. The magic arises when you lose yourself in your partner only to find yourself. Now that the main theme—passionate sex—is playing out romantically and joyously, you can reach orgasm.

You have arrived at the peak of ecstatic union, so how do you maintain the ardor? There's nothing like novelty, spontaneity, adventure to keep the excitement alive.

Brain chemistry climbs on board to enhance your excitement. The dopamine rush, along with testosterone, endogenous opioids, vasopressin, and oxytocin, brings the eroticism of lovemaking to unimaginable heights. Go with the erotic feeling wherever and whenever it bubbles up.

Your mirror neurons not only activate brain chemistry to enhance love and lust but also trigger nonverbal communication. When you vary the times, places, and positions of lovemaking, your partner's mirror neurons will reflect those changes, and he will join you. If he brings his own suggestions on how to enhance sex, your mirror neurons will reflect those suggestions, and you may well join him. Here are some suggestions to revive the lust:

- If you used to reserve lovemaking for after the dishes were done, leave them in the sink. Let spontaneity take over—make love in the morning, in the middle of the night, or at dusk.

- A tad of the forbidden can be adventurous and exciting. Park your car in a secluded place and make love in the backseat.

- The sun can do wonders to stimulate sexual desire. Surrender to the feelings and invite your partner to skinny-dip with you. A lake, the ocean, the swimming pool, or any romantic place can become a hot spot.

- For stimulating positions of lovemaking, there's nothing like the imagination. Imagine ways your partner can excite you sexually and how you can express your sexual desire for him. By talking to each other, you can't help but raise the level of eroticism.

- Then there is the aphrodisiac of novelty. Don't stay with the same missionary position. Try new positions. Let your partner know exactly what turns you on. If you are not sure, ask your partner to experiment, touching and kissing different parts of your body.

Acting on all of this brings erotic excitement, culminating in the deepest and most intimate of experiences.

Orgasm, whether simultaneous with your partner or not, is the climax of the performance. You have now rekindled the flame of desire with brain chemicals washing over your partner and you.

THE FINAL CURTAIN

Let's move to after the climax. Once you have experienced the ecstasy of orgasm, is that all there is? Not in the least! There's a lot more. You can maintain intimacy for the long haul. Remember, lasting love without lust is hardly true intimacy, just as lasting lust without love is not true intimacy.

It's what you feel and do now that count. Experience the feelings of oneness, of complete immersion in your partner. Once the flame of passion dies down, slow-burning coals continue to provide a soft, warm afterglow. Allow the warmth to permeate your body and your mind, and reach out with affection to your partner. Kiss, hold each other, whisper amorous words. Your matching mirror neurons will trigger the brain chemicals that promote attachment, loyalty, good moods, affection, and love.

How do you feel about all of this closeness? Can you surrender to tender feelings, or does part of you still fear intimacy? My hope is that, at this point—after working on problems in the relationship—you feel free to abandon yourself fully to real intimacy. Once the hot flame of desire arouses erotic passion, an ebbing of sexual desire leaves a blanket of delicious warmth. But this is hardly the end point of love. And that's because there are no end points in real love, only new beginnings.

You and your partner are headed in a new direction, toward a new beginning. Your path lies in between tensions—committed love and erotica, security and excitement, continuity and novelty, safety and adventure, comfort and passion.

There will, no doubt, be many other beginnings that extend into the beyond. It is in that space that the magic of lovers—with tensions, conflicts, love, and eroticism—continues to connect, disconnect, and reconnect again into infinity.

Just as there are no endings in love, the end of this book is only a beginning. You can continue from here. You and your partner can rewire your mirror neurons to reflect new heights, ever-new beginnings, and ever-lasting intimacy.

Endnotes

PART ONE

1. Doidge, N. (2007). *The brain that changes itself.* New York: Penguin Books.

CHAPTER ONE

2. Marazziti D., and Cassano, G. B. (2003). The neurobiology of attraction. *Journal of Endocrinol Invest* 26, 58–60.

3. Galesse, V., Fadiga, L., Fogassi, L., and Rizzolatti, G. (1996). Action recognition in the premotor cortex. *Brain* 119, 593–609.

4. Wolf, N. S., Gales, M., Shane, E., and Shane, M. (2000). Mirror neurons, procedural learning, and

the positive new experience. *Journal of the Academy of Psychoanalysis* 28, 409–430.

5. Graziano, M. S. A., and Gross, C. G. (1994). The representation of extrapersonal space: A possible role of bimodal visual-tactile neurons. In Grazsaniga, M. S. (ed.). *The Cognitive Neurosciences.* Cambridge, MA: MIT Press, 1021–1034.

6. Marazziti, D., and Cassano, G. B. (2004). Hormonal changes when falling in love. *Psychoneuroendocrinology* 29, 931–936.

7. Marazziti, D., and Cassano, G. B. (2003). The neuro-biology of attraction. *Journal of Endocrinol Invest* 26, 58–60.

8. Carter, C. S. (1998). Neuroendocrine perspectives on social attachment and love. *Psychoneuroendocrinology* 23, 779–818.

9. Marazziti, D., and Cassano, G. B. (2004). Hormonal changes when falling in love. *Psychoneuroendocrinology* 29, 931–936.

10. Carter, C. S. (1998). Neuroendocrine perspectives on social attachment and love. *Psychoneuroendocrinology* 23, 779–818.

11. Esch, T., and Stephano, G. B. (2004). The neurobiol-ogy of pleasure, reward processes, addiction and their

health implications. *Neuroendocrinology Letters* 25, 235–251.

12. Esch, T., and Stephano, G. B. (2005). The neurobiology of love. *Neuroendocrinology Letters* 26, 175–192.

13. Ficchione, G. L., Mendoza, A., and Stephano, G. B. (1994). Morphine and its psychiatric implications. *Advances in Neuroimmunology* 4, 117–132.

14. Ficchione, G. L., and Stephano, G. B. (2005). Placebo neural systems: Nitric oxide, morphine, and the dopamine brain reward and motivation circuitries. *Medical Science Monitor* 22, MS54–MS65.

15. Bartele, A., and Zeki, S. (2003). The neural correlates of maternal and romantic love. *NeuroImage* 21, 1155–1166.

16. Rizzolatti, G., and Arbib, M. (1998). Language within our grasp. *Trends in Neuroscience* 21, 188–194.

17. Ono, T., Nishijo, H., and Uwanao, T. (1995). Amygdala, role in conditioned associative learning. *Progress in Neurobiology* 46, 401–422.

18. Umitla, M. A., Kohler, E., Gallese, V., Fogassi, L., Fadiga, L., Keysers, C., et al. (2001). I know what you are doing: A neurophysiological study. *Neuron* 31, 155–165.

19. Fadiga, L., Fogassi, L., Pavesi, G., and Rizzolatti, G. (1995). Motor facilitation during action observation: A magnetic stimulation study. *Journal of Neurophysiology* 73, 2608–2611.

20. Gangitano, M., Mottaghy, F. F., and Pascual-Leone, A. (2001). Phase specific modulation of cortical motor output during movement observation. *NeuroReport* 12, 1489–1492.

21. Rizzokatti G., and Craighero, L. (2004). The mirror-neuron system. *Annual Review of Neuroscience* 27, 169–192.

22. Pally, R. (1997). How brain development is shaped by genetic and environmental factors: Developments in related fields of neuroscience. *International Journal of Psychoanalysis* 78, 587–593.

23. Udin, L., Kaplan, J., Molnar-Szakacs, I., Zaidel, E., & Iacoboni, M. (Submitted). Self-recognition activates a frontoparietal "mirror" network in the right hemisphere: An event-related fMRI study. *NeuroImage*.

24. Graziano, M. S. A., and Gross, C. G. (1994). The representation of extrapersonal space: A possible role for bimodal visual-tactile neurons. In M. S. Grazsaniga (ed.), *The Cognitive Neurosciences*. Cambridge, MA: MIT Press, 1021–1034.

25. Wolf, N. S., Gales, M., Shane, E., and Shane, M. (2001). The developmental trajectory from amodal perception to empathy and communication. *Psychoanalytic Inquiry* 21, 94–112.

26. Galesse, V., and Goldman, A. (1998). Mirror neurons and the simulation theory of mind-reading. *Trends in Cognitive Sciences* 2, 493–501.

27. Galesse, V. (2003). The roots of empathy: The shared manifold hypothesis and the neural basis of intersubjectivity. *Psychopathology* 36, 171–180.

28. Buckley, Cara. (January 3, 2007). Man is rescued by stranger on subway tracks. *New York Times.* www.nytimes.com/2007/01/03/nyregion/03life.html?ref=carabuckley.

29. Buckley, Cara. (January 7, 2007). Why our hero leapt onto the tracks and we might not. *New York Times.* www.nytimes.com/2007/01/07/weekinreview/07buckley.html.

30. Galesse, V. (2003). The roots of empathy: The shared manifold hypothesis and the neural basis of intersubjectivity. *Psychopathology* 36, 171–180.

31. Vollm, B. A., Alexander Taylor, N. W., Richardson, P., Corcoran, R., Stirling, J., McKie, S., et al. (2006). Neural correlates of theory of mind and empathy: A

functional magnetic resonance imaging study in a nonverbal task. *NeuroImage* 29, 90–98.

32. Hollander, E., Cartwright, C., Wong, C. M., De Caria, C. M., Del Giudice-Asch, G., Buchsbaum, M. S., and Aronowitz, B. R. (1998). A dimensional approach to the autism spectrum. *International Journal of Neuropsychology* 3, 22–39.

33. Oberman, L. M., Hubbard, E. M., McCleery, J. P., Altschuler, E. L., Ramachandran, V. S., and Pineda, J. A. (2005). EEG evidence for mirror neuron dysfunction in autism spectrum disorders. *Cognitive Brain Research* 24, 190–198.

34. Mobbs, D., Lau, H. C., Jones, O. D., and Frith, C. D. (2007). Law, responsibility, and the brain. *PLoS Biology* 5, 693–700.

35. Freud, S. (1958). *The dynamics of transference*. London: Hogarth Press.

36. Loewald, H. W. (1960). On the therapeutic action of psychoanalysis. *International Journal of Psychoanalysis* 41, 16–33.

CHAPTER TWO

37. Cozolino, L. (2002). *The neuroscience of psychotherapy: Building and rebuilding the human brain*. New York: Norton.

38. Casper, A., and Spence, M.(1986). Prenatal maternal speech influences newborn's perception of speech sound. *Infant Behavior and Development* 9, 133–150.

39. Shore, A. N. (1994). *Affect regulation and the origin of the self.* Hillsdale, NJ: Erlbaum.

40. Shore, A. N. (1996). The experience-dependent maturation of a regulatory system in the orbital prefrontal cortex and the origin of developmental psychopathology. *Development and Psychopathology* 8, 59–87

41. Wolf, N. S., Gales, M., Shane, E., and Shane, M. (2000). Mirror neurons, procedural learning, and the positive new experience. *Journal of the American Academy of Psychoanalysis* 28, 409–240.

42. Wolf, N. S., Gales, M., Shane, E., and Shane, M. (2001). The developmental trajectory from amodal perception to empathy and communication. *Psychoanalytic Inquiry* 21, 94–112.

43. Nelson, E. E., and Panksepp, J. (1998). Brain substrates of infant-mother attachment: Contributions of opioids, oxytocin, and norepinephrine. *Neuroscience and Biobehavioral Reviews* 22, 437–452.

44. Barteles, A., and Zeki, S. (2003). The neural correlates of maternal and romantic love. *NeuroImage* 21, 1155–1166.

45. Nelson, E. E., and Panksepp, J. (1998). Brain substrates of infant-mother attachment: Contributions of opioids, oxytocin, and norepinephrine. *Neuroscience and Biobehavioral Reviews* 22, 437–452.

46. Beebe, B., and Lachmann, F. M. (1998). Co-constructing inner and relational processes: Self and mutual regulation in infant research and adult treatment. *Psychoanalytic Psychology* 15, 480–516.

47. Beebe, B., Lachmann, F. M., and Jaffe, J. (1997). Mother-infant interaction structures and presymbolic self and object representations. *Psychoanalytic Psychology* 5, 305–337.

48. Beebe, B., and Lachmann, F. M. (1988). The contributions of mother-infant mutual influence to the origins of self and object representations. *Psychoanalytic Psychology* 5, 305–337.

49. Beebe, B., and Lachmann, F. M. (1998). Co-constructing inner and relational processes. Self and mutual regulation in infant research and adult treatment. *Psychoanalytic Psychology* 15, 480–516.

50. Crown, C. (1991). Coordinated interpersonal timing of vision and voice as a function of interpersonal attraction. *Journal of Language and Social Psychology* 10, 29–46.

51. Beebe, B., and Lachmann, F. M. (1988). The contributions of mother-infant mutual influence to the origins of self and object representations. *Psychoanalytic Psychology* 5, 305–337.

52. Emde, R. (1988). Development terminable and interminable: Innate and motivational factors from infancy. *International Journal of Psychoanalysis* 69, 23–42.

53. Lichtenburg, J. D. (1996). Caregiver-infant, analyst-analsyand exchanges: Models of interaction. *Psychoanalytic Inquiry* 16, 54–66.

54. Brennan, K., and Shaver, P. (1995). Dimensions of adult attachment, affect regulation, and romantic functioning. *Personality and Social Psychology Bulletin* 21, 267–283.

55. Bowlby, J. (1969). *Attachment and loss* (vol. 1). New York: Basic Books.

56. Ainsworth, K., Blehar, M., Waters, E., and Walls, S. (1978). *Patterns of attachment.* Hillsdale, NJ: Lawrence Erlbaum.

57. Tronick, E. (1989). Emotions and emotional communication in infants. *American Psychology* 44, 112–119.

58. Wolf, N. S., Gales, M., Shane, E., and Shane, M. (2000). Mirror neurons, procedural learning, and

the positive new experience. *Journal of the American Academy of Psychoanalysis* 28, 409–430.

CHAPTER THREE

59. Freud, S. (1958). *The dynamics of transference.* London: Hogarth Press.

60. Loewald, H. W. (1960). On the therapeutic action of psycho-analysis. *International Journal of Psychoanalysis* 41, 16–33.

CHAPTER FIVE

61. Ekman, P. (1992). Facial expressions of emotions: An old controversy and new findings. *Philosophical Transitions, Biological Sciences* 3, 1273.

CHAPTER SIX

62. Farrow, T. F. D., Zheng, Y., Wilkinson, I. D., Spence, S. A., Deakin, J. F. W., Tarrier, N., Griffiths, P. D., and Woodruff, P. W. (2001). Investigating the functional anatomy of empathy and forgiveness. *NeuroReport* 12, 2433–2438.

63. Konstarm, V., Holmes, W. S., and Levine, B. (2003). Empathy, selfism, and coping as elements of psychology of forgiveness: A preliminary study. *Counseling and Values*, 47.

64. Van Oyen Witvliet, C., Ludwig, T. E., and Vander Laan, K. L. (2001). Granting forgiveness or harboring grudges: Implications for emotion, physiology, and health. Personal correspondence with Charlotte van OyenWitvliet, Psychology Department, Hope College, Holland, MI.

CHAPTER SEVEN

65. Maroda, K. J. (2004). A relational perspective on women and power. *Psychoanalytic Psychology* 21, 428–435.

66. Doidge, N. (2007). *The Brain that Changes Itself.* New York: Penguin Books.

CHAPTER EIGHT

67. Klein, M. (1946). Notes on some schizoid mechanisms. *International Journal of Psychoanalysis* 1, 44–49.

68. Ogden, T. H. (1979). On projective identification. *International Journal of Psychoanalysis* 60, 357–373.

About the Author

Photo by Anthony Gallego

Dr. Fran Cohen Praver, a clinical psychologist and psychoanalyst, has been treating patients in her private practice for nearly two decades. A specialist in intimate relationships and their neuroscientific underpinnings, unconscious processes, trauma, and mood disorders, Dr. Cohen Praver is passionate about helping couples change their dynamics of pain to those of lasting love.

The author of *Crossroads at Midlife* (Praeger, 2004) and *Daring Wives: Insight into Women's Desires for Extramarital Affairs* (Praeger, 2006), Dr. Cohen Praver blogs for *Psychology Today* and has made television and radio appearances. She lives and practices in Long Island, New York.